Collins

Cambridge Lower Secondary

English as a Second Language

STAGE 7: WORKBOOK

T0340399

Nick Coates

William Collins' dream of knowledge for all began with the publication of his first book in 1819.

A self-educated mill worker, he not only enriched millions of lives, but also founded a flourishing publishing house. Today, staying true to this spirit, Collins books are packed with inspiration, innovation and practical expertise. They place you at the centre of a world of possibility and give you exactly what you need to explore it.

Collins. Freedom to teach.

Published by Collins
An imprint of HarperCollins*Publishers*
The News Building
1 London Bridge Street
London
SE1 9GF

HarperCollins*Publishers*
Macken House, 39/40 Mayor Street Upper,
Dublin 1, D01 C9W8,
Ireland

Browse the complete Collins catalogue at
www.collins.co.uk

© HarperCollins*Publishers* Limited 2021
10 9 8 7 6

ISBN 978-0-00-836685-8

British Library Cataloguing-in-Publication Data

A catalogue record for this publication is available from the British Library.

Author: Nick Coates
Series Editor: Nick Coates
Development editor: Helen King
Product Manager: Lucy Cooper
Project manager: Lucy Hobbs
Proof-reader: Sue Chapple
Cover designer: Gordon MacGlip
Cover illustrator: Maria Herbert-Liew
Typesetter: Jouve India Private Ltd
Production controller: Lyndsey Rogers
Printed and bound by: Ashford Colour Press Ltd.

MIX
Paper | Supporting responsible forestry
FSC™ C007454

This book is produced from independently certified FSC™ paper to ensure responsible forest management.

For more information visit: www.harpercollins.co.uk/green

Acknowledgements

The publishers gratefully acknowledge the permission granted to reproduce the copyright material in this book. Every effort has been made to trace copyright holders and to obtain their permission for the use of copyright material. The publishers will gladly receive any information enabling them to rectify any error or omission at the first opportunity.

Key: t = top, b = bottom, l = left, r = right, c = centre.

p11 Koto Moto/Shutterstock, p16 photokup/ Shutterstock, p17 Aurora72/Shutterstock, p25 HitToon/ Shutterstock, p26 chrisdorney/Shutterstock, p27 MikeBiTa/Shutterstock, p29 Jozef Klopacka/ Shutterstock, p42 domnitsky/Shutterstock, p46 Mykola Komarovskyy/Shutterstock, p49 BlueRingMedia/ Shutterstock, p49 Teguh Mujiono/Shutterstock, p49 Sunny_nsk/Shutterstock, p53 Laura Pl/Shutterstock, p57 Sam72/Shutterstock, p60 Albina Glisic/Shutterstock, p63 MichaelJayBerlin/Shutterstock, p64 Roobcio/ Shutterstock, p74 Yodchompoo/Shutterstock, p76tl WICHAI WONGJONGJAIHAN/Shutterstock, p76tc Venus Angel/Shutterstock, p76tr mhatzapa/ Shutterstock, p76bl SeDmi/Shutterstock, p76bc TrifonenkoIvan/Shutterstock, p76br Marques/ Shutterstock, p77 Everett Historical/Shutterstock, p78 Alones/Shutterstock, p81 La Gorda/Shutterstock, p88 Lemonade Serenade/Shutterstock.

With thanks to the following teachers and schools for reviewing materials in development: Hawar International School; Khushnuma Gandhi, HVB Global Academy; Judith Hughes, International School of Budapest; Babara Khan, Jankidevi Public School.

Contents

Introduction

The Collins *Cambridge Lower Secondary English as a Second Language* course consists of a Student's Book and Workbook for students for each of Stages 7, 8 and 9. A Teacher's Guide includes other lesson ideas and materials, and your teacher will also have access to the recorded listening materials.

The *Stage 7 Workbook* directly supports the Student's Book with a Workbook unit for every unit in the Student's Book. The units are numbered in the same way and the sequence of activities in the Workbook follow those of the Student's Book. Each Workbook activity also has a page reference to the relevant activity in the Student's Book to make the link between the two books clear. The Workbook units give you further practice of the grammar, vocabulary and skills taught in the Student's Book. It also contains activities designed either for support or for extension work. For example, to accompany the Student's Book reading activities, the Workbook includes *Reading: comprehension* and *Reading: thinking about the text* activities. The *comprehension* activity can be used for further practice of basic comprehension. The Workbook *thinking about the text* activity focuses on more advanced reading skills such as implied meaning, critical analysis and application, so you can use it to challenge yourself. The *Focus on Grammar* section at the back of the Workbook provides a short summary of the key grammar points for Stage 7 which you can use for reference.

For teachers

Registered Cambridge International Schools benefit from high-quality programmes, assessments and a wide range of support so that teachers can effectively deliver Cambridge Lower Secondary. Visit www.cambridgeinternational.org/lowersecondary to find out more.

1 Language and communication

Reading: comprehension

SB p.10

1 Which language is spoken in the most countries?

   a Chinese   **b** English   **c** Spanish

2 Which language has the most mother tongue speakers?

   a Chinese   **b** English   **c** Spanish

3 What is a world language?_____

4 Which language must all pilots learn?_____

Reading: thinking about meaning

SB p.10

1 Why are world languages important?

_____

2 Why do you think people don't know how many languages there are in the world?

_____

3 Why can't we say which language is the most important?

_____

Reading: using a dictionary

SB p.11

Finding the meaning of a word in a dictionary:

- If you use a dictionary in book form, remember that it lists the words in alphabetical order. The better you know the English alphabet, the quicker you can find a word in a dictionary.

Write these words in alphabetical order.

- If two words start with the same letter, look at the second letter.
- If two words start with the same first two letters, look at the third letter, and so on.

1 Anika   Paulo   Femi   Lin   _____   _____   _____   _____

2 Chinese   English   French   Russian   Spanish   Arabic

_____   _____   _____   _____   _____   _____

3 Africa   Asia   America   Antarctica   _____   _____   _____   _____

4 English   England   Chinese   China   _____   _____   _____   _____

5 continent   country   communicate   conversation

_____   _____   _____   _____

1 Label the continents on the map.

| Africa   Antarctica   Asia   Oceania   Europe   North America   South America |

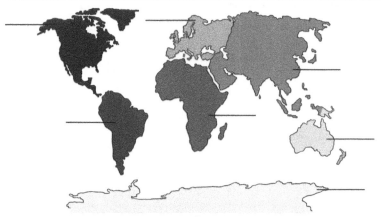

Vocabulary: nationalities

We make the words for **nationalities** from the names of the countries.

most end in –*(i)an*   American, Australian, Egyptian, Russian

some end in –*ese*   Chinese, Japanese, Portuguese

some end in –*ish*   British, English, Spanish

but   French (from France)

Most words for **languages** are the same as nationalities.

     English people speak English in England. Russians speak Russian in Russia.

but

     Arab people live in various countries and speak Arabic.

Complete the table and add to it.

Country	Nationality	Language
England	English	1 _____
Australia	2 _____	Australian
3 _____	Spanish	4 _____
Egypt	5 _____	Arabic
6 _____	Chinese	7 _____
France	8 _____	French
9 _____	10 _____	11 _____
12 _____	13 _____	14 _____

Vocabulary: languages

SB pp.10–11

Write the names of different languages to make a word picture like the one on page 10 in your Student's Book.

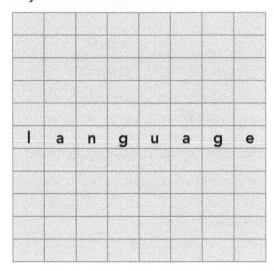

l	a	n	g	u	a	g	e

Use of English: pronouns

SB p.12

1 Complete the sentences with the pronouns from the box.

> someone   anything   no one   everything   anyone   everyone

1 Do you know _____ who lives in London?

2 The classroom is empty – there's _____ here.

3 Be quiet! I heard _____ talking.

4 Do you want _____ to drink?

5 The children were here but _____ has gone home now.

6 My school bag fell in the river. I lost _____ .

2 The words in the box can be used as pronouns that tell us about quantity. Complete the sentences with the correct pronoun.

> none   a few   less   more   all

1 I asked my friends to meet me but _____ of them have arrived!

2 A: Where are the girls?

B: They're _____ outside playing basketball.

3 A: Are any languages used in more than one country?

B: Oh, yes, there are _____ .

4 A: Are all the students in the classroom now?

B: Not yet, _____ are coming soon.

5 There's a lot of noise in here! Can I have _____ , please?

Use *have / has* + past participle of the verb.

Put *not* after *has / have* to make the negative form.

I		walked.
You	have ('ve)	arrived.
We	have not	known.
They	(haven't)	seen.

He		walked.
She	has ('s)	arrived.
It	has not	known.
	(hasn't)	seen.

The past participle of a regular verb is the same as the past tense form. It ends in -ed.

There are many common verbs with irregular past participles. You have to learn these.

1 Complete the sentences with *has, hasn't, have* or *haven't*.

1 We *have* just walked here from home.

2 Where is Nahla? She *hasn't* arrived at school.

3 I _____ just met your brother.

4 Ben is here. He _____ just arrived.

5 Anika _____ just changed her dress. The other one was blue.

6 It's windy in here because we _____ closed the door.

7 Musa _____ spoken to me today. I think he's angry with me.

8 This film is new. I _____ seen it before.

2 Complete the sentences with past participles from the box. Use *just*.

| broken | ~~washed~~ | cut | picked |

1 She *has just washed* her hair.

2 He _____ his leg.

3 They _____ flowers.

4 Somebody _____ a window.

Use of English: past participles

Write the past participles of the verbs. Use a dictionary, if necessary. Then complete the crossword.

Clues

Across

1 bring _____

3 leave _____

6 draw _____

7 speak _____

9 fall _____

11 understand _____

12 teach _____

Down

2 ride _____

4 forget _____

5 choose _____

8 mean _____

10 keep _____

Check your progress

1 What can you do now?

I can ...

express opinions about language learning □

write a conversation □

find important information in a text □

name some continents, countries, nationalities and languages □

use tone of voice to express feelings □

talk about the recent past using the present perfect tense □

💡 **My learning**

What did you learn in this unit?

2 Answer the questions about this unit.

1 What have you enjoyed most?

_____

2 Is there anything you have found difficult?

_____

3 What would you like to learn more about?

_____

Reading: comprehension SB p.18

Read the text about different types of shops once more. Are the sentences true, false, or doesn't the text say?

1 Mini-markets are often expensive.	True / False / Doesn't say
2 You will find many specialist stores in supermarkets.	True / False / Doesn't say
3 Most people use shopping malls.	True / False / Doesn't say
4 Markets have been in use for hundreds of years.	True / False / Doesn't say
5 Specialist shops are bigger than department stores.	True / False / Doesn't say
6 Internet shopping is now the most popular type of shopping.	True / False / Doesn't say

Reading: thinking about the text SB p.18

1 Can you think of any differences between these types of shops?

1 supermarket / mini-market   *A supermarket has more products and is cheaper.*

2 market / supermarket   _____

3 mini-market / internet shopping   _____

4 specialist shop / shopping mall   _____

2 Can you think of any similarities between these types of shops?

1 supermarket / mini-market   *They both have a lot of products.*

2 department store / shopping mall   _____

3 market / speciality shop   _____

4 internet shopping / shopping mall   _____

Vocabulary: shopping SB p.19

1 Find five words we can use to talk about shops and shopping.

n	s	t	o	r	e	r	w
k	u	k	p	j	m	v	m
m	g	q	c	f	g	c	a
a	t	d	h	g	q	f	r
l	y	f	o	r	z	r	k
l	h	t	i	w	d	t	e
c	h	e	c	k	o	u	t
w	m	s	e	s	d	f	g

_____

_____

_____

_____

_____

2 Complete the sentences with the words from the box.

> checkout   convenient   experience   huge   products   self-service   specialist

There is a mini-market that is very ¹_____ for me because it is on the way to school. In the past, there was a man who gave you what you wanted. But now the shop is ²_____. You have to find the ³_____ you want and then take them to the man at the ⁴_____ so that you can pay. It's OK, but I prefer small ⁵_____ shops because they are more friendly and interesting than ⁶_____ supermarkets or department stores. They give you a better ⁷_____.

Use of English: talking about quantity

SB pp.19–20

Some words describing quantity can be used only with countable nouns or with uncountable nouns. Other words describing quantity can be used with both countable and uncountable nouns. For more information, look at the section on Quantifiers on page 95 for help.

1 Choose the correct word.

1 How *many / much* water is there?
2 Can I have *a few / a little* onions, please?
3 I have *several / a little* money, but I need more to buy what I want.
4 There is *plenty of / many* coffee if you want some.
5 I've got *a large number of / a large amount of* books. Do you want any?
6 There are *several / a little* shoe shops in the mall.

2 Use the words to write new sentences.

1 plenty of   _____
2 several   _____
3 a large amount of _____
4 a large number of _____

1 Look at the pairs of sentences. Do they mean the same thing or are they different?

1 My brother is older than me.   same / different

I'm not as old as my brother.

2 The market is cheaper than the supermarket.   same / different

The market is not as cheap as the supermarket.

3 It's quicker to walk to school than to go by bus.   same / different

Walking to school is not as quick as going by bus.

4 The jewellery in the department store is better than in   same / different
the mall.

The jewellery in the mall is not as good as in the department
store.

2 For each pair of sentences with different meanings in 1 above, rewrite the second
sentence so that it has the same meaning.

_____

_____

_____

_____

3 Rewrite each sentence so that it has the same meaning, using *not as … as …* and
the same adjective.

1 Russia is bigger than China.
China is not as big as Russia.

2 Flying is cheaper than travelling by ship.

_____

3 Taxis are more convenient than buses.

_____

4 You are funnier than your brother.

_____

5 My new phone is bigger than my old one.

_____

Use of English: idioms

SB p.21

Match the idioms with their meaning.

1	to see eye to eye	**a**	to get something correct
2	to cost an arm and a leg	**b**	to feel ill
3	to cut corners	**c**	to do things quickly and badly
4	to hit the nail on the head	**d**	to be very expensive
5	to feel under the weather	**e**	to agree with someone

Use of English: *have to*

SB p.21

Complete the sentences with the correct form of *have to*.

1 Ray _____ go to hospital yesterday.

2 My younger sister always _____ go to bed at seven o'clock.

3 We _____ leave early tomorrow to get there on time.

4 What time _____ you _____ go home?

5 What time _____ you usually _____ get up in the mornings?

Writing: punctuating speech

SB p.23

1 Write the missing punctuation.

"Hello__" said Maria.

"Hello, Maria, it's Dad. Where are you?__ asked Dad.

Maria said, "I'm shopping__"

2 Write all of the missing punctuation for the rest of the conversation.

Dad said We're going to eat soon. You have to come home

OK said Maria I'll be there in ten minutes

Please don't be late said Dad

Maria answered I won't

Reading: finding information fast

Sometimes you can find information in a text very easily and quickly. If you want to find a number or a date in a part of the text, you can:

- first look at the headings to find the part of the text that you need
- then run your eyes over the text, looking only for numbers.

You don't need to read every word.

Look at the text and find the answers quickly.

1 How many people work at Kejetia market? _____

2 How many stores are there in the Grand Bazaar? _____

3 How many shops and stalls are there in Kejetia market? _____

4 When was the Grand Bazaar built? _____

Check your progress

1 What can you do now?

I can …

talk and write about different types of shops ☐

compare things using not as … as … ☐

listen and understand the main points in conversations ☐

take part in a role play ☐

write a conversation based on the role play ☐

discuss the advantages and disadvantages of different shops ☐

2 Answer the questions about this unit.

1 What have you enjoyed most?

_____

2 Is there anything you have found difficult?

_____

3 What would you like to learn more about?

_____

💡 My learning

What did you learn in this unit?

Reading: using a dictionary

SB p.30

Sometimes when you look up a word in a dictionary you might not understand the definition. A good dictionary always includes an example sentence. This helps to make the meaning clearer and shows how to use the word.

word you look up

part of speech

irregular form

definition

thief noun (*thieves*)

a person who steals something from another person: *The thieves took his camera.*

example sentence

Look up these words in a dictionary and find the example sentences.

word	example sentence
thief	*The thieves took his camera.*
prison	
arrest	
lawyer	

Vocabulary: crimes

SB p.30

Find 10 words we can use to talk about crime.

b	p	o	l	i	c	e	k	x	o	p	l
r	g	h	j	k	y	v	n	m	f	q	w
t	r	q	s	z	x	f	g	t	f	c	v
h	h	a	c	k	e	r	y	d	i	c	s
i	t	y	j	l	p	l	c	s	c	w	t
e	t	n	a	x	c	n	w	z	e	r	e
f	p	c	r	t	r	i	a	l	r	m	a
p	r	x	r	w	d	f	r	t	h	b	l
l	i	q	e	j	l	a	w	y	e	r	k
w	s	w	s	t	f	b	j	u	o	p	k
d	o	b	t	w	q	x	g	t	h	j	m
x	n	m	w	r	p	i	r	a	t	e	v

Reading: comprehension

SB p.31

1 Read again the report about Jo Jones. Put these events in the correct order.

a arrested	**c** fell asleep	**e** prison	**g** woke up
b broke in	**d** had tea	**f** trial	

1 _____ 2 _____ 3 _____ 4 _____

5 _____ 6 _____ 7 _____

2 Read again the report about Ivan Conti's trial. What three things did the police find?

_____ _____ _____

Reading: thinking about the text

SB p.31

1 What is unusual about what Jo Jones did? Why do you think he did it?

_____

2 Why do you think the girl hacked into the school computer?

_____

3 What do you think the pirates will do with Ali Modi?

_____

4 Where do you think Ivan Conti got the laptop, mobile phones and handbag from?

_____

Vocabulary: more crime words

SB p.32

1 Match the words with their meanings.

1 arrest	**a** a person who does something that is against the law
2 criminal	**b** a person whose job it is to help people with the law and speak for them in a trial
3 hacker	**c** take someone to a police station because they have done something wrong
4 lawyer	**d** a formal meeting where people decide if someone has committed a crime
5 trial	**e** a person who uses a computer to get information from another person's computer

2 Complete the sentences with the words from the box.

broke into   prison   report   reward   thieves

1 There was a _____ on the TV news about a crime.

2 Some criminals _____ a bank and stole $30 000.

3 The boss of the bank offered a _____ to anyone who helped catch the criminals.

4 They were caught and sent to _____ for 10 years.

5 Two _____ stopped me in the street and stole my car.

Use of English: the passive

SB pp.32–33

1 Complete the passive sentences.

ACTIVE	PASSIVE
1 Someone broke the glass.	The glass _was broken_.
2 They cleaned the classroom yesterday.	The classroom _____ yesterday.
3 Millions of people watched the Olympic Games.	The Olympic Games _____ by millions of people.
4 My brother didn't use this computer much.	This computer _____ much.
5 Someone in Italy made these shoes.	These shoes _____ in Italy.
6 Nobody saw us.	We _____ by anybody.

2 Rewrite the sentences using the passive form. Don't use *by ....*

1 Someone took her bicycle.   _Her bicycle was taken._

2 The police didn't arrest the thieves.

_____

3 A man asked me for directions.

_____

4 They built this school about 50 years ago.

_____

5 A teacher found this wallet in the dining room.

_____

6 Someone took me to hospital after my accident.

_____

We often have to change pronouns when we report speech:

*Ali said, "I am late." → Ali said that **he** was late.*

1 Complete the reported speech with the correct pronouns.

1 Usman said, "We are waiting." → Usman said that _____ were waiting.

2 Maria said, "I want to see Fatima." → Maria said that _____ wanted to see Fatima.

3 Abel said, "I have lost my cap." → Abel said that _____ had lost _____ cap.

4 The children said, "We won our match." → The children said that _____ had won _____ match.

We also have to change some 'time and place' words:

*Ali said, "It's here now." → Ali said that it was **there then**.*

*See examples of how time and place words change in **Focus on Grammar**, Section 8 on pages 91–92.*

2 Complete the reported speech.

1 "I want to see you now." → He said that he wanted to see me _____.

2 "I'm going out today." → George said that he was going out _____.

3 "We met Julia last week." → They said that they had met Julia _____.

4 "We want to meet here." → They said that they wanted to meet _____.

5 "What are you doing tomorrow?" → He asked me what I was doing _____.

6 "I lost my dictionary last month." → He said that he had lost his dictionary _____.

When we report something that was said in the past, we have to make changes to the verb tenses.

*See how verb tenses change in **Focus on Grammar**, Section 8 on pages 91–92.*

3 Choose the correct verb tense to complete the sentences.

1 "I'm feeling better."   She said that she *was feeling / had felt* better.

2 "We like our swimming lessons."   They said that they *liked / had liked* their swimming lessons.

3 "We tried to help." The man said that they *tried / had tried* to help.
4 "Dina has just gone out." She said that Dina *just went / had just gone* out.
5 "I'm going for a swim." He said that he *is going / was going* for a swim.
6 "We broke the chair." She said that they *have broken / had broken* the chair.

Writing: spelling and punctuation

SB p.35

1 Find five mistakes in this paragraph.

Teenage detective James Mbenzi is travelling to england by plane. During the journey, a pasenger is robbed of all his money. someone on the flight knows what happend, but who would want to rob an old man? How is it possible that no one saw it happen.

2 Write the paragraph correctly.

_____

_____

_____

_____

Check your progress

1 What can you do now?

I can ...

talk about crime and criminals ☐

find information in newspaper reports and police reports ☐

use the passive to say what was done ☐

report what people said ☐

write a police report ☐

write a book blurb ☐

2 Answer the questions about this unit.

1 What was the most interesting part?

_____

2 Is there anything you didn't like?

_____

3 What would you like to learn more about?

_____

My learning

What did you learn in this unit?

Reading: comprehension   SB p.41

Read the text and decide if the sentences are true or false.

1 A Komodo dragon is bigger than a person.   True / False
2 They kill a lot of children.   True / False
3 They run after animals to kill them.   True / False
4 They eat dead animals.   True / False
5 They eat a lot of burgers.   True / False
6 They are reptiles.   True / False

Reading: thinking about the text   SB p.41

Read the text again and answer the questions.

1 Why do Komodo dragons follow animals after they bite them?

   _____

2 How much meat can a Komodo dragon eat in one meal?

   _____

3 Why will you probably not meet a Komodo dragon?

   _____

4 Are Komodo dragons the biggest reptiles in the world?

   _____

Vocabulary: words in context   SB p.42

1 Complete the sentences with the words from the box.

bacteria	bit	creatures	escaped	lay	live	scary	sharp

1 We _____ in a house near the river.

2 Like all _____, reptiles need water.

3 Our chickens _____ eggs on most days.

4 The thief _____ from prison before his trial.

5 This film is too _____ for young children.

6 We need a _____ knife to cut plastic.

7 Everyone got ill because there were dangerous _____ in the water.

8 Fiona _____ into her sandwich.

2 Match the adjectives and the nouns.

adjectives	nouns
high	depth
long	height
wide	length
deep	width

3 The five nouns in the box can be used to talk about size. Use them to complete the paragraph.

weight	depth	height	length	width

There's a wonderful swimming pool in our town. It's big! It has a ¹_____ of 50 metres and a ²_____ of 20 metres. At one end, the ³_____ is only 1 metre and children can play safely. However, the other end is much deeper, so that adults can jump or dive in. There's a board for diving from at a ⁴_____ of 5 metres above the pool. What I really like is that in water my body doesn't feel heavy. The water helps to hold up the ⁵_____ of my body.

Use of English: the present perfect with *for* and *since*

1 Complete the sentences with *for* or *since*.

1 We have lived here _____ three years.

2 She has been out _____ six o'clock this morning.

3 My uncle has been ill _____ a long time.

4 Have you seen Amina _____ last week?

5 He has played the guitar _____ he was five years old.

6 Have you known Bintu _____ very long?

2 Write complete sentences. Use the present perfect tense.

a Iris / live / in that house / since she was born
   Iris has lived in that house since she was born.

b I / have / this laptop / since my birthday

   _____

c I / know / Salma / for three years

   _____

d We / be / friends / since we were born

   _____

e They / not eat / for 24 hours

   _____

Use of English: *can* and *could*

SB p.43

When we talk about possibility in the present, or ability in the present, we use *can* or *can't*. The past of *can* and *can't* is *could* and *couldn't*.

Complete the sentences with *can, can't, could* or *couldn't*.

1 Elephants _____ live for 80 years.

2 I _____ go to see Komodo dragons before, because I didn't have enough money to travel to Indonesia.

3 Komodo dragons _____ fly.

4 The film about dragons was great. I _____ understand everything that they said.

5 _____ your brother play the guitar? No, he _____ .

6 _____ you swim when you were six years old? No, I _____ .

Vocabulary: living things

SB p.44

1 Complete the diagram with the words from the box.

birds	dragonfly	fish	Komodo dragon
rabbit	reptiles		

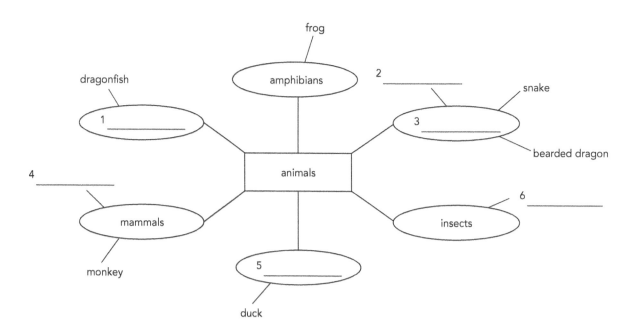

2 Add to the diagram. Write the names of any other animals you know, in the correct places.

Writing: personal experience

Write sentences to answer the questions.

1 When do you light candles?

_____

2 Do you like fireworks? When do you see them?

_____

3 Who do you know that wears red?

_____

4 What do you like doing at New Year?

_____

Use of English: reported speech with *said* and *told*

1 Complete the sentences with *said* or *told*.

1 I _____ that I can't hear you.

2 I _____ you that I can't hear you.

3 Julia _____ that she was writing a letter.

4 The teacher _____ us that tomorrow is a holiday.

5 The boys _____ the doctor that there had been an accident.

6 We _____ that we were very happy to hear the news.

2 Complete the reported speech.

1 We enjoyed the story.   The children _____

2 You can leave.   The teacher _____ us _____

3 I'm afraid of monsters.   Julio _____

4 I want you to go.   She _____ them _____

Read the clues and complete the crossword about Chinese New Year. You can find all the words in the text.

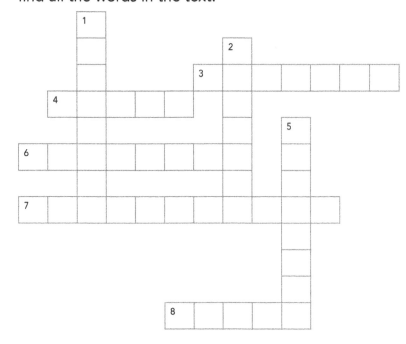

Across

3 to get ready
4 a long thin piece of wood
6 flat paper you send a letter in
7 a party or fun event for a special reason
8 to make someone or something afraid

Down

1 a time when people celebrate a special event
2 a gift: something nice you give to someone
5 to make something look attractive or beautiful

Check your progress

1 What can you do now?

I can ...

find key facts about an animal from a webpage ☐

talk about the unfinished past using the present perfect, *since* and *for* ☐

write a webpage about an animal ☐

listen to and then retell a story ☐

work with others to write about a festival ☐

read and understand a folk tale ☐

2 Answer the questions about this unit.

1 What have you learned?

_____

2 Is there anything you have found difficult?

_____

3 What would you like to learn more about?

_____

My learning

What did you learn in this unit?

Reading: comprehension

SB p.53

What is the newspaper report about? Match the sentence parts.

1 All three stories in the newspaper report are about
2 The three works of art were
3 However, all the cleaners made
4 They didn't know the rubbish or the dirty bath were
5 So they did their job and

a cleaned them away.
b cleaners and works of art.
c not the same.
d the same mistake.
e works of art.

Reading: thinking about the text

SB p.53

1 Read the newspaper report again. Describe the differences between the works of art by Gustav Metzger and Damien Hirst.

_____

_____

2 Which of these statements do you most agree with? Explain why.

● *Modern art is rubbish.*

● *Cleaners don't understand modern art.*

● *Modern art is fun and can make us laugh.*

_____

_____

3 Do you think the artists were angry with the cleaners? Explain why you think this.

_____

_____

Vocabulary: words in context

SB pp.53–54

1 Complete the sentences with words from the box.

| bin   collection   mistake   pile of rubbish   studio |

1 I think Damien Hirst's _____ must be very dirty and untidy.

2 I've made a terrible _____ ! I've thrown away my paint brush.

3 My uncle has a huge _____ of toy cars. He's collected them since he was a boy.

4 Can you clean your bedroom, please? There's a _____ behind the bed.

5 Collect all the rubbish and throw it in the _____ , please.

2 Choose the best word to complete the sentences.

1 Tate Britain and Eyestorm are _____ in London. [collections / displays / galleries]

2 There's an interesting _____ of paintings and sculpture in the school art room. Let's go to have a look. [exhibition / gallery / studio]

3 My paints are finished. I need to _____ them. [collect / replace / tidy]

4 I'm going to make a _____ of all my paintings and try to sell some. [display / gallery / pile]

Use of English: revision

SB pp.53–54

Read the newspaper report again.

1 Find two examples of the present perfect tense.

_____   _____

2 Find two examples of the past passive with *by*.

_____   _____

3 Find one example of the past passive without *by*.

_____

Use of English: relative clauses

SB pp.54–55

Complete the sentences with the relative clauses from the box.

which I did in our last art lesson	which I see every day on my way to school
which is quite new	who also teaches us science
~~who is from China~~	who was a famous painter

1 Suzy, *who is from China*, speaks Chinese, English and French.

2 Our car, _____ , doesn't start when it's cold.

3 Our head teacher, _____ , is going to talk to us all tomorrow.

4 My painting, _____ , is on display in the library.

5 Vincent van Gogh, _____ , had a very difficult life.

6 The sculpture, _____ , is made from old plastic and other rubbish.

Use of English: relative clauses with *whose*

> We can also use *whose* to start a relative clause.
>
> It shows possession and replaces *his, her, its* or *their*.

Join the two sentences to make one longer sentence.

1 Modi has a cinema in her home. Her father is a businessman.
Modi, whose father is a businessman, has a cinema in her home.

2 My friend Stefan travels a lot. His mother is from Russia.

_____

3 Our neighbours are always very busy. Their new house is being built.

_____

4 I think the worker did what he thought was right. His job was to clean the gallery.

_____

5 The artist made a lot of huge sculptures. I can't remember his name.

_____

Vocabulary: words in context

SB p.56

1 Listen to the talk and match the words with their meanings.

1 branch	**a** the glass part of a lamp that gives out light
2 bulb	**b** a piece of equipment used to reach high places
3 ladder	**c** one of the parts of a tree that grow from the trunk
4 attention	**d** when you look at something and think about it carefully

2 Complete the sentences. Use the correct form of the words in question 1 above.

1 We need a _____ to get up on the roof.

2 Read this and give it your full _____. It is important!

3 We need to replace the _____ because the lamp isn't working.

4 A _____ broke off a tree in the wind yesterday and hit a car.

Vocabulary: abstract nouns

1 Find six abstract nouns in the paragraph. Underline them.

We went to see a great film last night. It was about how hate can make people bad. But it was also about how love can make people better. It was very exciting and funny at times. In one scene some children broke the law by driving a car very fast. But the police made a mistake and arrested the wrong people. At the end, the children found happiness. It made us feel that there is hope in a difficult and dangerous world.

2 Write two more abstract nouns.

_____   _____

Now use them in new sentences.

_____

_____

_____

_____

Use of English: *like* and *as*

It can help us to understand things if we compare them to something else.

We can use *like* + noun to make comparisons, e.g. *It's a strange painting. It's like a dream*.

1 Use your own words to complete the descriptions. Use verb + *like* + noun.

1 The painter works like _____

2 The display looks _____

3 The studio _____

We can also describe things by comparing them to other things using *as* + adjective + *as* + noun.

The painting is as strange as a dream.   *Damien Hirst's studio is as dirty as a pile of rubbish.*

2 Use your own words to complete the descriptions. Use *as* + adjective + *as* + noun.

1 The gallery was as quiet as _____

2 The sculpture is as _____

3 The artist was _____

Vocabulary: a quiz

SB pp.51–60

1. Which 'b' word is where you put rubbish?

   _____

2. Which 'd' word is a collection of paintings or other works of art for people to look at? _____

3. Which 'g' word is where art is shown? _____

4. Which 'm' word is something you remember from the past?

   _____

5. Which 'm' word is something you didn't mean to do?

   _____

6. Which 's' word is where an artist works?

   _____

7. Choose three photos of works of art from this unit that you like. Give them names.

   _____   _____   _____

8. What type of art do you like doing? _____

Check your progress

1 What can you do now?

I can …

talk about art using appropriate vocabulary ☐

read and discuss a newspaper report ☐

make my sentences more interesting by using relative clauses ☐

talk and write about a painting ☐

express some feelings, thoughts and opinions about works of art ☐

identify a favourite work of art and encourage others to like it ☐

My learning
What did you learn in this unit?

2 Answer the questions about this unit.

1 What have you enjoyed most?

   _____

2 Is there anything you have found difficult?

   _____

3 What would you like to learn more about?

   _____

Reading: comprehension SB p.62

Read the text again and complete the table.

	high speed	team sport	lots of rules	water sport
kitesurfing	✓	✗		
skydiving				
white-water rafting				

Reading: thinking about the text SB p.62

1 Which of the three sports is the fastest? _____

2 Which is the slowest? _____

3 What are the dangers of each of the sports?

  1 kitesurfing _____

  2 skydiving _____

  3 white-water rafting _____

4 Which of the sports do you think is the most exciting? Give your reasons. _____

_____

Vocabulary: words in context SB p.63

Complete the sentences using the words from the box.

| aim   excitement   pouring   rock   rules   speed |

1 All schools have _____ so that students know what they must and mustn't do.

2 He drove down the mountain road at great _____ – we were really afraid!

3 The passengers were in great danger after the ship hit a _____ .

4 The water is _____ off the houses into the street.

5 There was a lot of _____ when they won the competition for the third time.

6 We _____ to make all our customers happy.

Vocabulary: adventure sports

1 Write the names of the sports under the pictures.

diving	diving	kitesurfing	skiing	skydiving
snowboarding	surfing	waterskiing	windsurfing	

1 _____

2 _____

3 _____

4 _____

5 _____

6 _____

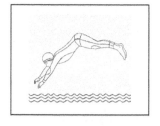

7 _____

8 _____

9 _____

2 Have you ever done any of these sports? If so, how did it make you feel?

_____

3 Which of these sports would you like to try? Why?

_____

4 What other adventure sports can you name? Make a list.

_____

Vocabulary: more compound nouns

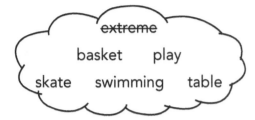

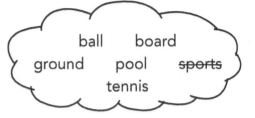

1 Match words from each cloud to make six more compound names of sports and games or places you can do them. Are they one word (*snowboarding*) or two words (*mountain biking*)?

2 Write a meaning for each word. Use a dictionary, if necessary.
Extreme sports: a sport that is exciting and maybe dangerous (also adventure sports).

1 _____

2 _____

3 _____

4 _____

5 _____

Vocabulary: compound adjectives

A *compound adjective* is a word which describes a noun and is made up of two (or more) words. The words are joined by a hyphen, for example: half-price, well-known.

1 Can you find a compound adjective in the text? Which noun does it describe?

_____

2 Complete the sentences with the compound adjectives from the box.

beautiful-smelling	English-speaking	never-ending
good-looking	slow-moving	

1 That's a _____ hat. I think I'll buy it.

2 These _____ flowers are my favourites.

3 There are many _____ countries in the world.

4 It was a very _____ film. I found it rather boring.

5 I feel sorry for my aunt and uncle because their problems are _____.

Speaking: pronunciation of compound words SB p.65

In compound words, one of the words is given more stress (said with more force) than the other.

In compound nouns, the stress is on the first word, e.g. 'skateboard, 'basketball.

In compound adjectives, the stress is on the second word, e.g. fast-'moving, good-'looking

Mark the stress. Say the words.

1 windsurf **2** well-known **3** half-price **4** swimming pool

Vocabulary: word families

Words in the same family have the same main part and related meaning.

- *Diving in the deep sea is exciting but dangerous.* Diving is a noun. It is an activity.
- *You can learn to dive in a swimming pool.* Dive is a verb. It is an action.
- *I know a diver who found an old ship.* Diver is a noun. It is a person.

1 Complete the table.

activity (noun)	action (verb)	person (noun)
diving	dive	**1** _____
surfing	**2** _____	surfer
snowboarding	snowboard	**3** _____
4 _____	ski	skier

2 Choose the correct word to complete the sentences.

1 My friends all love _____ but I prefer snowboarding. [skiing / ski / skier]

2 I want to learn to _____ next year – it looks really cool! [snowboarding / snowboard / snowboarder]

3 We're going to _____ at the weekend if the weather is good. [surfing / surf / surfer]

4 My brother's a champion _____. He's going to a competition in the USA next year. [skateboarding / skateboard / skateboarder]

5 I never want to _____. You won't get me to jump out of a plane! [skydiving / skydive / skydiver]

6 Did you see that _____? She just fell in the water. [waterskiing / waterski / waterskier]

Use the table to make four more sentences.

1 I'm tired	about	coming to the skate park with me?
2 We talked	at	hitting your boat when we were sailing.
3 Are you interested	for	skiing.
4 I'm sorry	in	waiting for the wind.
5 My brother's very good	of	windsurfing all evening.

1 *I'm tired of waiting for the wind.*

2 _____

3 _____

4 _____

5 _____

Check your progress

1 What can you do now?

I can …

find important information in a text ☐

name eight adventure sports ☐

understand and use some compound nouns ☐

find important information when I listen to an interview ☐

write about an adventure sport ☐

plan and write a timetable ☐

2 Answer the questions about this unit.

1 What have you enjoyed most?

_____

2 Is there anything you have found difficult?

_____

3 What would you like to learn more about?

_____

My learning

What did you learn in this unit?

Vocabulary: transport

SB p.74

Add words to the diagram from your discussion in *Speaking: word race* in your Student's Book.

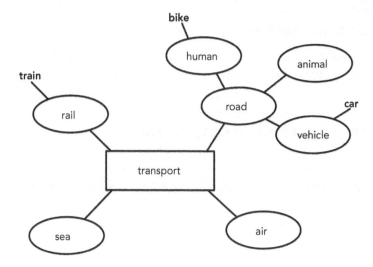

Vocabulary: words in context

SB p.75

Choose the best word to complete the sentences.

1 We don't have any _____, so of course the car won't go. [fuel / power]

2 Today people can get _____ from the wind, the Sun and from water. [fuel / power]

3 We will see you when you _____. [arrive / arrival]

4 We will see you on your _____. [arrive / arrival]

Use of English: connectives

SB p.75

Connectives connect two ideas.

- Some connectives always go **between** the two ideas (for example, *and, or, but, so*).
- Other connectives can go **between** the two ideas or at the **beginning** of the sentence. If it is at the beginning of a sentence, use a comma to separate the two ideas.
  Although *I like flying, I didn't enjoy that journey.*

1 Complete the sentences with *and, or, but, so, because, although*.

1 The bus will leave at 11 o'clock, _____ don't be late.

2 We stopped work _____ it was too hot.

3 _____ it was very hot, we were able to keep working.

4 I am going to have a drink _____ something to eat when I get home.

5 I made you some tea _____ you didn't drink it.

6 It doesn't matter if they come _____ not.

2 Join the sentences, using the connective. In some cases, more than one correct answer is possible.

1 I was tired. I ran home. [although]

   *Although I was tired, I ran home. / I ran home although I was tired.*_____

2 I need your help. I don't know what to do. [because]

   _____

3 I need your help. I don't know what to do. [so]

   _____

4 Do you want to go home now? Do you want to go home later? [or]

   _____

5 I'm tired. I don't want to go to bed. [but]

   _____

6 We played well. We lost the game. [although]

   _____

Use of English: *as* and *therefore*   SB p.75

Complete the second sentence so that it means the same as the first sentence.
Use *as* or *therefore*.

1 The plane is slow because it gets its power from the Sun.

   *As it gets its power from the Sun, the plane is slow.*_____

2 The pilot had to stay in his seat all the time because there was no space to stand up.

   There was no space, _____ the pilot _____.

3 Planes can fly without fuel because they can get power from the Sun.

   As planes can _____.

4 The pilot only slept for 20 minutes at a time because he had to fly the plane.

   As the pilot _____ , he _____

5 The pilot was very tired when he landed because he had to fly for five days and nights across the Pacific Ocean.

   The pilot _____ for five days and nights, _____

Reading: comprehension

SB p.77

1 Read the text again and decide if the sentences are true or false.

1 Petrol engines pollute the environment.   True / False
2 Electric cars need a battery.   True / False
3 Hybrid cars use electric and hydrogen engines.   True / False
4 Hydrogen cars have to carry oxygen.   True / False
5 Solar cars use less petrol than normal cars.   True / False
6 The author knows what cars will be like in the future.   True / False

2 Rewrite the false sentences to make them true.

_____

_____

_____

Reading: thinking about the text

SB p.77

1 Which of these adjectives would you use to describe the text? Use a dictionary, if necessary.

interesting / attractive / useful / confusing

2 What do you think are the advantages and disadvantages of an infographic text?

_____

_____

3 What sort of information can you put in an infographic text?

_____

Vocabulary: words in context

SB p.78

Complete the sentences with the words from the box.

| burn   continue   plug … in   produce   reduce |

1 Driving slowly can _____ the amount of pollution.

2 I think the car companies will start to _____ more hydrogen cars one day.

3 The battery on my phone has no power – I need to _____ it _____ .

4 We mustn't stop to rest yet – we need to _____ until we get there.

5 We could _____ this wood to get warm.

Use of English: *will, [be] going to*

SB p.78

- We use *will* + verb when we are talking about our ideas, opinions or predictions about the future, **without** evidence.
- We use *[be] going to* + verb when we have a plan for the future or when we are talking about our ideas, opinions or predictions, **with** evidence.

1 Choose the best way to complete the sentences.

1 Look at the clouds! It *will / is going to* rain soon.

2 I think the roads *will / are going to* be dangerous if it keeps raining.

3 I hope my mother *will / is going to* like the present I bought her.

4 We *will / are going to* have a party next Saturday.

5 A: I think I *will / am going to* paint this chair.

B: Really? What colour *will you / are you going to* paint it?

2 Use your own words to complete these sentences about the future.

1 I think there will be _____.

2 There's going to be _____.

3 I believe _____.

4 I know _____.

Reading: understanding the text

SB p.80

Read the text and choose the correct answer.

1 Urbanisation is when people move …

a from the countryside to towns and cities.

b from towns and cities to the countryside.

2 There is more work for people in …

a rural areas.　　　　　　　　　　b urban areas.

3 The UK is …

a an urban society.　　　　　　　b a rural society.

4 Many people choose to live …

a in the centre of cities.　　　　　b on the edge of cities.

5 Those people drive to the centre of cities …

a to go to work.　　　　　　　　b to go home.

6 Congestion is when …

a there is a lot of slow traffic.　　b traffic stops moving.

Vocabulary: crossword

Read the clues and complete the crossword about urbanisation and traffic management.

Across

1 work that you are paid for

6 when the roads and streets are very busy, we get …

8 the opposite of *wide*

9 an area with a special purpose

10 to make something happen

Down

2 a very wide road that lets cars travel fast

3 the part of something that is furthest from the centre

4 all the people who live in a country or an area

5 the answer to a problem

7 vehicles (for example, cars, taxis, buses) in the road

Check your progress

1 What can you do now?

I can …

identify facts when listening to a news report ☐

use some connectives ☐

find information in an infographic ☐

talk about the future of transport ☐

write information for an infographic ☐

2 Answer the questions about this unit.

1 What did you find the most interesting?

_____

2 What would you like to learn more about?

_____

3 Is there anything you have found difficult?

_____

My learning

What did you learn in this unit?

Reading: comprehension SB p.84

Order the sentences to tell the story of stone soup.

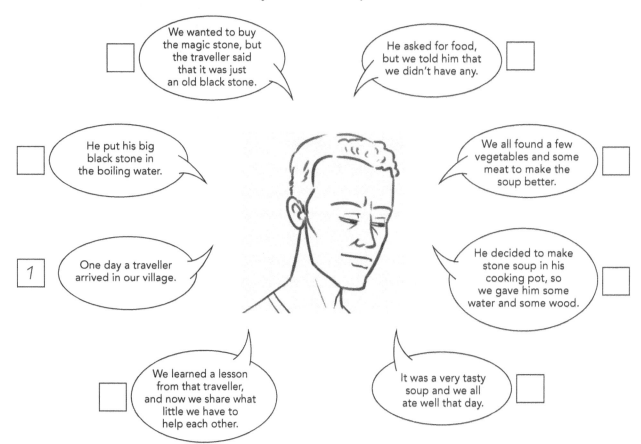

We wanted to buy the magic stone, but the traveller said that it was just an old black stone. ☐

He asked for food, but we told him that we didn't have any. ☐

He put his big black stone in the boiling water. ☐

We all found a few vegetables and some meat to make the soup better. ☐

One day a traveller arrived in our village. 1

He decided to make stone soup in his cooking pot, so we gave him some water and some wood. ☐

We learned a lesson from that traveller, and now we share what little we have to help each other. ☐

It was a very tasty soup and we all ate well that day. ☐

Vocabulary: words in context SB pp.84–85

Complete the sentences with the words from the box. Change the form where necessary.

| drop   ingredients   smell   stir   tasty   thick |

1 Cook the soup until it is _____ like cream.

2 In my opinion, to make a _____ soup you must always use a lot of pepper.

3 The food _____ wonderful – it made me feel hungry.

4 The soup needs to be _____ every 15 minutes.

5 Tom _____ the ball out of the window onto the car below.

6 We have most of the _____ for the cake but we still need some eggs.

1 Put the questions into reported speech. Use *if.*

  1 "Does your friend like soup?"   Mother asked if my friend _____.

  2 "Is Femi going to get water?"   The teacher asked if Femi _____.

  3 "Can you collect some wood?"   The traveller _____.

  4 "Have you ever eaten stone soup?"   Jo _____.

  5 "Did you break the window?"   Father _____.

  6 "Will he be here tomorrow?"   The teacher _____.

2 Put the questions into reported speech. Use the question-word, not *if.*

  1 "Where did the traveller sleep?"   The teacher asked _____.

  2 "When will the soup be ready?"   The children asked _____.

  3 "Why are we waiting?"   Femi _____.

  4 "Who can remember the story?"   Our teacher _____.

  5 "What time are you going out?"   Mother _____.

  6 "How many games do you have?   My father _____.

3 Think of three questions you have asked a friend this week. Report your questions.

I asked Maria if she would share her lunch with me. _____

_____

_____

Now think of three questions that people asked you this week. Report the questions.

Ella asked me to help her with her project. _____

_____

_____

1 Match the different types of stories with the descriptions.

  1 crime   **a** about people and events that make you laugh

  2 romance   **b** about exciting, unusual and maybe dangerous events

  3 adventure   **c** about life and adventures in the future

  4 humour   **d** about things and events that frighten you

  5 science fiction   **e** about criminals and the police catching them

  6 biography   **f** about love and relationships

  7 horror   **g** about the life of a real person

2 Which one of the types of stories above is non-fiction? _____

Reading: comprehension

SB p.87

Match the questions and answers.

1 Jan told me that you are writing a story. What's it about?

a Don tells the story himself. That means it's told using 'I' and 'me' rather than 'he' and 'his'. I find this is a good structure because it means I can write all of Don's thoughts and ideas.

2 Who is this character?

3 Is the story easy to read?

4 Oh, where is it set, then?

5 It sounds great! What else can you say about the story?

b His name is Don – he doesn't have any other name.

c In South America, about a hundred years ago.

d It's about how a cruel and bad man learns to be good. It has a serious and important theme.

e Oh, yes, because the plot is very simple. Don goes on a long and dangerous journey down a river and through a forest.

Vocabulary: words in context

SB p.87

Complete the text with the words from the box.

| action challenge character events perfect plot setting theme |

I've just finished reading a great story which I think everyone should read. It's easy to read because it has a very simple
¹_____. It starts when the main
²_____ (he's called Eric) is born and it follows him though his whole life. Not a lot happens. The only
³_____ is when he goes away to fight in a war for a few years. For the

rest of the book, the ⁴_____ is a small village in England, from 1920 to 1999 – and it's a very quiet village! There are very few exciting ⁵_____ in Eric's life but he's not a boring man. Eric's not ⁶_____ – he's sometimes unkind to his family – but he tries his best. The only ⁷_____ he faces is that he has been very poor all his life but he never let that worry him.

I know the story sounds uninteresting but I was never bored when I read it. It's written beautifully and I loved the ⁸_____. The message it gives is that a simple life can be good and interesting. Eric may not have any money but he's rich in many other ways!

Writing: using the text

SB p.87

Think about a favourite story and complete the table.

Characters	
Setting	
Plot beginning	
middle	
end	
Theme (or lesson)	

Use of English: adjectives ending in –*ing* and –*ed*

SB p.88

1 Choose the correct adjective.

1 My uncle is very *amused / amusing* when he tells stories.

2 I went on a very *tired / tiring* run this morning.

3 I've been working all day and now I'm *exhausted / exhausting*.

4 My younger brother never leaves me alone. He's very *annoyed / annoying*.

5 I can't do this exercise – I am *confused / confusing*.

6 The bus driver's driving was terrible, so we had a *frightened / frightening* journey.

2 Make your own sentences with the phrases below.

a annoying child   *All afternoon, the annoying child asked, 'Why? Why? Why?'* _____

confusing journey   _____

bored engineer   _____

worried birds   _____

amazing afternoon   _____

Writing: a kenning poem

1 Read the poem about a teacher and the information about kenning poems.

Book reader
Board writer
Loud talker
Work checker
Spell corrector
Homework setter
Child helper

A kenning is a two-word phrase that describes something without actually naming it (for example, *word keeper* for a dictionary). Kenning poems use a list of different kennings to describe a subject without naming it.

2 What do you think these kenning poems are about?

Team player **1** _____

Ball passer

Long kicker

Strong tackler

Fast runner

Throw-in taker

Goal scorer

People connector **2** _____

Message taker

Number recorder

Text sender

Information bringer

Photo taker

Time teller

Alarm ringer

Music player

3 Write your own kenning poem.
- Think of a subject you want to write about. The subject can be a person, an object or anything else you like.
- Make notes about what the subject does or looks like.
- Write your poem. The lines are short, usually only two words, but you can make them a bit longer.
- Read your poem to a friend. Can they guess the subject?

Check your progress

1 What can you do now?

I can ...

listen to and follow a long story ☐

report questions ☐

name the main elements of a story ☐

write an exciting opening to a story ☐

understand and talk about some short poems ☐

create and write a story in a group ☐

My learning

What did you learn in this unit?

2 Answer the questions about this unit.

1 What have you enjoyed most?

_____

2 Is there anything you have found difficult?

_____

3 What would you like to learn more about?

_____

Mid-year review

Vocabulary: word hunt

SB pp.93–98

Write three words that are:

1 the names of continents

2 things sold in a pharmacy

3 acts done by criminals

4 the names of things in art galleries

5 the names of water sports

6 forms of sea transport

Vocabulary: a crossword

Follow the clues to complete the crossword puzzle.

Across

1 a small object that gives power for things such as a mobile phone

4 someone whose job is to find out what happened in a crime and who did the crime

9 the opposite of 10 across

10 very old, or from a long time ago

Down

2 something that happens to you

3 a meeting in which someone asks another person, often someone famous, questions about their life or work

5 a person who does something against the law

6 to make something look attractive or beautiful

7 to make less or smaller

8 to find an answer to a problem

Writing: punctuation

Read and correct the punctuation.

Once, many years ago there lived an old woman in a small village. she was very poor but she did own two goats. Every morning she took the goats down the road to the fields One morning two young men who thought they were very clever saw the old woman with her goats.

"Good morning, mother of goats! they shouted.

The old woman smiled at them and said "good morning, my sons"

Writing: using the correct word

Some words sound the same but have a different spelling and a different meaning. Some of these words are used a lot, so it is important that you use the correct spelling.

1 Rewrite the sentences, correcting the spelling.

   1 What are you going to where?   *What are you going to wear?*

   2 Where is there house?   _____

   3 I new you were going to ask that.   _____

   4 These shoes are two small for me.   _____

   5 Your not sure what to do, are you?   _____

   6 I can't here the teacher very well.   _____

2 Write your own sentences using these words.

   1 a meet   _____

     b meat   _____

   2 a write   _____

     b right   _____

   3 a poor   _____

     b pour   _____

9 Wildlife under threat

Vocabulary: words in context

SB p.100

Complete the sentences with the words from the box.

diseases hunted increase intelligent land net ocean skin

1 The farmer uses some of the _____ for animals and the rest for food crops.
2 An elephant has thick, grey, very strong _____.
3 My sister is very _____ but she doesn't work hard enough.
4 Smoking causes several _____ and can kill you.
5 There has been an _____ in the number of elephant hunters in southern Africa.
6 Tigers are _____ for their beautiful skins.
7 When they pulled the _____ out of the sea, it was full of fish.
8 You fly across the _____ when you go to Australia.

Use of English: modal verbs

SB p.101

1 Read the sentences and then answer the questions.

A: *We must do something to help the gorillas.*   B: *What can we do?*
A: *Should we stop cutting down their forests?*   B: *We could try.*

1 Can modal verbs have more than one form (for example, *musts, musting, musted*)?
2 Do we use *do, does* or *did* in questions with modals (for example, *Do I can go now*)?
3 Do we use the simple form of a main verb (without *to*) after a modal (for example, *You should work hard.*)?

2 Find four incorrect sentences, then write them correctly.

1 Does Anton might arrive today?
2 Yes, and he will to see you when he gets here.
3 Shouldn't we help the others?
4 An hour ago we coulded see the Moon but now we can't see it.
5 What can I tell my mother when she asks where we were?
6 It's getting late, so you must to hurry up.

_____

_____

_____

_____

Reading: comprehension

SB p.102

Read the text again. Are the sentences true, false, or doesn't the text say?

1 In 1925 there were 10 000 cheetahs in Namibia.   True / False / Doesn't say
2 Cheetahs often live near to people.   True / False / Doesn't say
3 Farmers killed 1000 cheetahs in 1994.   True / False / Doesn't say
4 Cheetahs live only in Namibia.   True / False / Doesn't say
5 The CCF dogs are stronger than cheetahs.   True / False / Doesn't say
6 Cheetahs in Namibia are now in less danger than   True / False / Doesn't say
   they were.

Reading: thinking about the text

SB p.102

1 Imagine there were no CCF dogs but farmers were told not to kill cheetahs. What do you think would happen?

_____

_____

2 What lesson can we learn from this CCF programme about protecting endangered animals?

_____

_____

Vocabulary: words in context

SB p.102

1 Complete the sentences with the words from the box.

| clever   fight   programme   protect   result   shoot   speed   successful |

   1 When cheetahs _____, they bite with their sharp teeth.

   2 I hope farmers don't _____ more cheetahs – it's sad!

   3 Everyone worked hard and at great _____ to finish quickly.

   4 I want to be a scientist but I don't know if I am _____ enough.

   5 The school swimming team had a very _____ year. They won all their competitions.

   6 Our school has a _____ to help more students take part in sports.

   7 The bus was late, as a _____ of an accident which closed the road.

2 Which word from the box is not used in the sentences above? Use this word to write a sentence of your own.

Writing: using noun phrases

1 Match the parts to make sentences.

1 Sometimes cheetahs hunt

2 Big dogs, which think of the sheep and goats as family, protect

3 This clever idea is now used

a the animals from cheetahs, which don't like to fight.

b in several other countries where cheetahs are found.

c farm animals that can't protect themselves.

2 Write sentences about the animals. Use noun phrases to add interest and information.

1 polar bear

2 panda

3 whale

Use of English: *so ... that* and *such ... that*

SB p.104

1 Complete the sentences with *so* or *such*.

1 The mountain gorilla is _____ a clever animal that it can use sign language.

2 The mountain gorillas are _____ endangered that you need permission to go to see them.

3 My sister talks _____ quietly that nobody can hear her.

4 Anika is _____ a clever woman that everyone wants to meet her.

5 I made _____ a terrible mistake that I failed my driving exam.

6 Those shoes are _____ expensive that I don't think anyone will buy them.

2 Join the two sentences with *so ... that* or *such ... that*.

1 It was a cold day outside. I closed the window.

It was such a cold day outside that I closed the window.

2 I was thirsty. I drank three cups of water.

_____

3 The plants were dry. I had to give them water.

_____

4 It is a young bird. It can't fly yet.

_____

5 I was lost. I had to ask for directions.

_____

6 It was a lot of money. I couldn't buy it.

_____

Use of English: *why* clauses

SB p.105

Complete the sentences with your own words.

1 The reason why I was late for school today is that _____.

2 The reason why some farmers want to shoot wild animals is that _____.

3 The reason why I didn't call you is that _____.

4 I was in hospital last week. That's why _____.

Vocabulary: Biology

SB p.106

Match the words to their meanings.

1 classify   a give food
2 feed   b plant or animal groups that are similar
3 species   c put people or things into groups

Reading: finding facts

SB p.106

Read the text again and complete the table.

	mammals	birds	fish	amphibians	reptiles
have lungs	✓	✓			
are cold-blooded					
are warm-blooded					

Check your progress

1 What can you do now?

I can ...

listen to find facts in a talk ☐

use different modal verbs (for example, *can, should, must*) ☐

find information in a text quickly ☐

use noun phrases to make my writing better ☐

take part in a meeting ☐

write a report of the meeting ☐

2 Answer the questions about this unit.

1 What have you enjoyed most?

_____

2 Is there anything you have found difficult?

_____

3 What would you like to learn more about?

_____

💡 My learning

What did you learn in this unit?

Reading: comprehension

SB p.110

Read the text again. Are the sentences true, false, or doesn't the text say?

1 The writer thinks there is no problem with climate change because Earth is still beautiful.   True / False / Doesn't say

2 Scientists are worried about changes in air temperature and sea levels.   True / False / Doesn't say

3 Air temperatures are now about 1°C higher than they were in 1880.   True / False / Doesn't say

4 In the last century, the sea level didn't go up at all.   True / False / Doesn't say

5 By the end of this century, the sea level will be much higher, and this will be dangerous for Earth.   True / False / Doesn't say

6 Water from melting glaciers increases the sea level.   True / False / Doesn't say

Reading: thinking about the text

SB p.110

1 The word *still* is used seven times in paragraph 1. Why do you think the writer did this?

_____

2 Why do you think the writer included the graph with the text?

_____

3 Read the last sentence. What do you think some of the changes in the future might be?

_____

_____

Vocabulary: words in context

SB p.110

1 Find in the text the words *increased* and *rose*.

1 The verb *increase* means *get bigger*. Can you name the verb for *get smaller*?

_____

2 The verb *rise* (past tense *rose*) means *go up*. Can you name the verb for *go down*?

_____

2 Complete the paragraph with the words from the box. Change the form where necessary.

> average   climate   glacier   issue   melt   rise   seem   tiny

People often talk about global
warming, but from day to day we don't
feel any change in temperature – it
¹_____ to stay the same.
However, when there is only a
²_____ increase in the
³_____ temperature
around the world, things start to
change. In many mountains, the
⁴_____ have started to
warm and then ⁵_____. The water runs into the seas which start to
⁶_____. This rise in water level can threaten the homes of people who live
near a river or the sea. So, ⁷_____ change is an ⁸_____ that is
important in all our lives.

Use of English: comparing with adverbs SB p.111

1 Complete the sentences with the adverbs from the box.

> far more happily   less loudly   much less carefully   not as heavily as   twice as well

1 He was driving _____ than usual when he had the accident.

2 The baby plays _____ now that his mother has come home.

3 He was very angry but he shouted _____ than he usually does.

4 The rain is pouring down but _____ it did last night.

5 Last time I played tennis, I did quite well but only won two games. This time I did
_____ because I won four games.

2 Use the adverbs to make your own sentences.

1 more quickly: _____

2 half as well as: _____

3 much more slowly: _____

Use of English: the likely conditional

SB p.113

> We use the likely conditional to talk about the result of events that are likely to happen in the future.
>
> For more information, see the section on *General and likely conditionals* in *Focus on Grammar* on page 91.

1 Choose the best way to complete the sentences.

   1 If my dad buys me a bike, I *cycle / will cycle* to school.

   2 If we get a cat, it *caught / will catch* the mice.

   3 I *buy / will buy* us some soft drinks if I can find my money.

   4 Anna *lend / will lend* you her hat if you *ask / will ask* her.

   5 If you *buy / will buy* a car, where *you go / will you go*?

2 Write the verbs in the correct form.

   1 We are looking for the key. If we <u>find</u> the key, we <u>will open</u> the door. [find, open]

   2 If you _____ , I _____ earlier. [want, come]

   3 They _____ their exams if they _____ harder. [pass, work]

   4 I don't know if I have any money. If I _____ some money, I _____ you some. [have, lend]

   5 If you _____ me some money, I will _____ you tomorrow. [lend, repay]

   6 I _____ you later if you _____ me your number. [call, give]

3 Rewrite the sentences with *unless*. They should have the same meaning.

   1 If you don't go to the party, I won't go.
     Unless you go to the party, I won't go.

   2 Amy won't get better if she doesn't go to hospital.

   _____

   3 A snake won't bite you if you don't move.

   _____

   4 Peter won't phone us if he doesn't need something important.

   _____

   5 We won't help you if you don't help us.

   _____

Reading: the greenhouse effect

Read the text and complete it with the words from the box.

building   causes   cold   escapes   inside   stronger   warmer

The greenhouse effect

A greenhouse is a [1] _____ made of glass. It has glass walls and a glass roof. When the sun shines, it gets very warm [2] _____ the greenhouse. At night, the glass keeps some of the heat inside, so it doesn't get too cold. Greenhouses are very useful for growing plants quickly.

The air around Earth (called the *atmosphere*) does the same as a greenhouse. During the day, the Sun shines and Earth warms up. At night, some of the heat [3] _____, but the atmosphere keeps some of it inside, so Earth doesn't get too [4] _____.

The problem these days is that carbon dioxide in the atmosphere is making the greenhouse effect [5] _____. Less heat can escape at night, so more stays inside. The world is slowly getting [6] _____. This increase in temperature [7] _____ climate change.

Vocabulary: multi-word verbs with *turn*

SB p.115

Complete the sentences using a multi-word verb with *turn*. For example: *turn off, turn up*.

1 _____ the television before you go to bed, please.

2 Don't _____ the lights unless you need to.

3 I can't hear the music, so can you _____ the radio, please.

4 In the story, a frog _____ a king.

5 Please _____ and look at the board.

6 We were all worried about the meeting but it all _____ well.

7 You can _____ the heating a bit to save energy.

8 You can now _____ your exam papers and start writing.

Vocabulary: a crossword

Read the clues and complete the crossword.

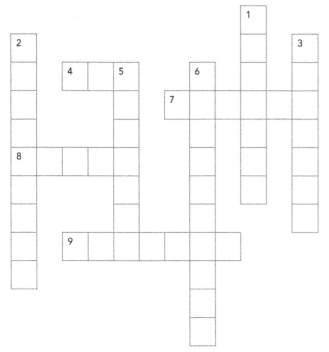

Across

4 the centre of a hurricane

7 a country in North America that is not the USA

8 the country that was hit by a monsoon in 2005, killing over a thousand people

9 a dangerous wind that spins very fast

Down

1 a disease carried by mosquitoes

2 another name for a typhoon or cyclone

3 a large area of ice that moves slowly down a mountain

5 an imaginary line around Earth

6 the country that was hit by the Bhola cyclone in 1970

Check your progress

1 What can you do now?

I can ...

make adverbs stronger or weaker ☐

use the likely conditional ☐

discuss ways to save energy ☐

write an article for a school magazine ☐

work with others to successfully create a poster ☐

2 Answer the questions about this unit.

1 What have you enjoyed most?

_____

2 Is there anything you have found difficult?

_____

3 What would you like to learn more about?

_____

My learning

What did you learn in this unit?

Healthy living

Vocabulary: words in context

SB pp.122–123

1 Complete the sentences with the words from the box.

> benefit   cause   diet   lecture
> nutrients   overweight   underweight

1 We had a very interesting _____ about plant-based diets yesterday.

2 We need _____ from food to help us grow and stay healthy.

3 I think the traditional Japanese _____ of rice, fish and vegetables is a healthy one.

4 A poor diet can _____ ill health.

5 When I was a baby, my parents were worried because I was _____. They gave me so much to eat that I was soon _____.

2 Which word from the box is not used? Use this word to write a sentence of your own.

_____

_____

Use of English: present perfect tense

SB p.123

Write sentences with the answers to the questions you asked your classmates.

Mina has never been a vegan but she is a vegetarian. She doesn't want animals killed for food.

_____

_____

_____

_____

_____

_____

_____

Use of English: idioms

SB p.124

Complete the sentences with the idioms in the box.

kill two birds with one stone	pull someone's leg
let the cat out of the bag	see eye to eye

1 "Maria and I are working in the same group for our project, but it just isn't working: we don't _____ on anything."

2 "We have to go shopping on Saturday, so you can go to see the dentist while we are in the city – then we can _____ "

3 "We told Abel that the head teacher wanted to see him, so he ran to the school office. He was really mad with us when he found out that we were _____ his _____ "

4 "My family wanted to give a surprise party for my dad, but my little sister _____. "

Reading: comprehension

SB p.126

Read the text again. Are the sentences true, false, or doesn't the text say?

1 If you eat healthy food, you will have a healthy lifestyle.   True / False / Doesn't say

2 Part of a healthy lifestyle is to exercise, to get enough sleep and to keep your teeth clean.   True / False / Doesn't say

3 You shouldn't eat any chips, sweets, cakes or anything with a lot of sugar in it.   True / False / Doesn't say

4 You should eat a lot of fruit and vegetables.   True / False / Doesn't say

5 The five top tips are given in the text in their order of importance.   True / False / Doesn't say

Reading: thinking about the text

SB p.126

1 What will happen if you do a lot of exercise and don't eat much? Is it healthy to do this every day?

_____

2 Why do you think you shouldn't eat sugary food or drinks before you go to bed?

_____

Use of English: talking about quantity

SB p.126

Look at the *Eat a balanced diet* tip from the text. Find and write six different ways to talk about the amount or quantity of something.

a lot of _____   _____

_____   _____

_____   _____

Vocabulary: abstract nouns

SB p.127

We can make abstract nouns from adjectives by adding *-ness*, e.g. *illness*. If the adjective ends in *y*, change it to an *i* before adding *-ness*, e.g. *happiness*.

Change these adjectives to abstract nouns.

1 fit _____   **2** healthy _____   **3** weak _____   **4** good _____

5 empty _____   **6** mad _____   **7** tidy _____   **8** sad _____

Vocabulary: words in context

SB p.127

1 Match the words with their meanings.

1 confused	**a** unusual or strange
2 surprising	**b** a useful piece of advice
3 sugary	**c** not able to understand something or think clearly about something
4 tip	**d** tasting sweet

2 Complete the sentences with the words in the box.

> balanced   confusing   energy   illness   surprised   surprising   tip

1 Our teacher gave us a useful _____ for the exam.

2 I find it very _____ when somebody says one thing one day and something different the next day.

3 Eating a bit of everything but not too much of anything is the key to a _____ diet.

4 I was so tired that I didn't have the _____ to get out of bed.

5 They were _____ when they saw me walk in the door: they thought I was in the USA.

6 Pablo is away from school because of _____.

3 Which word from the box is not used? Use this word to write a sentence of your own.

_____

Use of English: using the –*ing* form SB p.127

1 Complete the sentences about the text, using the words from the box.

| Making   Brushing   ~~Eating~~   Eating   Exercising   stopping |

1 *Eating* a balanced diet is good for you.

2 _____ when you're hungry and _____ when you are no longer hungry is a good tip.

3 _____ for about 60 minutes a day will help to keep you healthy.

4 _____ sure you get enough sleep is important.

5 _____ your teeth well will help you avoid some serious illnesses.

2 Read the A sentences, and complete the B sentences so that they have the same meaning. Use one or two words only.

1 A It's not easy to find a good job.

  B _____ a good job is not easy.

2 A It takes time to choose the best trainers.

  B _____ the best trainers takes time.

3 A I'll ask for help again.

  B I'll keep _____ for help.

4 A It is important to learn languages.

  B _____ is important.

5 A My grandfather is happy that he doesn't work now.

  B My grandfather enjoys _____ now.

> TAKE CARE
> *of your body*
> IT'S THE ONLY
> PLACE
> YOU HAVE
> *to live in*

Look at the healthy food plate to find the names of 10 fruits and vegetables.

d	r	t	v	g	r	a	p	e	s	o	t
m	t	u	h	k	l	m	c	p	a	j	o
u	r	l	e	m	o	n	e	k	p	k	m
s	d	s	f	p	w	y	l	m	p	m	a
h	s	l	v	k	s	g	e	n	l	n	t
r	x	e	c	n	x	b	r	v	e	h	o
o	c	t	b	j	c	n	y	a	q	v	p
o	z	t	n	c	u	c	u	m	b	e	r
m	q	u	b	m	v	v	x	d	j	x	d
p	e	c	p	i	n	e	a	p	p	l	e
g	g	e	v	d	b	s	c	f	h	w	w
b	a	n	a	n	a	q	r	c	g	q	r

Check your progress

1 What can you do now?

I can ...

follow a lecture and identify the main points ☐

talk about experiences using the present perfect with *ever* and *never* ☐

use some common idioms ☐

identify what is necessary for a healthy lifestyle ☐

write a questionnaire about healthy living ☐

My learning

What did you learn in this unit?

2 Answer the questions about this unit.

1 What have you enjoyed most?

_____

2 Is there anything you have found difficult?

_____

3 What would you like to learn more about?

_____

Reading: comprehension

SB p.132

Read the text again. Are the sentences true, false or doesn't the text say?

1. Each player is asked 12 questions.   True / False / Doesn't say
2. The first question is the most difficult.   True / False / Doesn't say
3. Major Ingram left the army after playing the game.   True / False / Doesn't say
4. Major Ingram won a lot of money so that he could   True / False / Doesn't say
   leave the army.
5. Major Ingram went to prison.   True / False / Doesn't say
6. *Slumdog Millionaire* was made before *Q&A* was written.   True / False / Doesn't say

Reading: thinking about the text

SB p.132

1. What evidence does the writer give to show *Who Wants to Be a Millionaire?* is the most popular show in the world?

   _____

2. Why do you think the writer used the phrase *from Afghanistan to Vietnam* when giving examples of countries that watch the show?

   _____

3. Do you think Major Ingram's plan to win the game show was a clever one?

   _____

Vocabulary: words in context

SB p.133

1. Complete the advert with the words from the box.

   audience   millionaire   reduced   series   successful

   Join in!
   An exciting new [1] _____ of 10 programmes starts on Sun TV next month. It's a quiz show in which the whole [2] _____ watching TV will answer questions using the internet. After each question, players with the wrong answer will not be able to continue. A [3] _____ number of players carry on answering questions. Anyone who is still in the game at the end of the show will be invited to play again the following week. If someone is still playing after three shows, the [4] _____ player will win a million dollars. Yes – this is a chance to become a [5] _____ while sitting on your sofa!

2 Complete the sentences with the words in the box.

> reach   soldiers   army   notice   cough

1 He knows a lot, so I think he will _____ the final part of the quiz.
2 The government thinks there won't be a war, so they want to reduce the size
  of the _____ . They are going to send about eight hundred
  _____ home.
3 People sometimes _____ to make other people _____ them.
  It's a way of saying, 'I'm here!'

Use of English: adding meaning

SB p.134

1 Underline the phrases starting with prepositions in the sentences.
1 Abel ran *around the corner*.
2 I saw it in the garden but I think it has gone now.
3 For over 50 years, she waited for her son to come home.
4 If we run fast we can hide under the bridge.
5 My father's gone to the bank but he'll be back soon.
6 You need to go down the road, past the school and then through the gate.

2 Complete the sentences with a preposition and phrase.

1 I'll race you *up the hill*.

2 I got this bike _____.

3 _____ , you can win a lot of money.

4 We haven't seen him _____ , but we'll see him tomorrow.

Vocabulary: word maker

Play this quiz show game. Make 12 new words from the letters in *game show*.

game show

game _____   *am* _____

_____   _____

_____   _____

_____   _____

_____   _____

_____   _____

Use of English: review of verb tenses

SB p.134

Choose the correct verb tense.

Who wants to be a Millionaire [1]<u>was shown</u> [shows / was shown] for the first time in the UK in 1998. Although the TV company [2]_____ [stopped / was stopped] it in 2014, it [3]_____ [is started / was started] again in 2018.

It now [4]_____ [has / had] a new lifeline and a new question master. The new lifeline [5]_____ [is / was] 'ask the host' which [6]_____ [means / has meant] that the player can [7]_____ [ask / asks] the question master for help. In the past, the new host [8]_____ [is / was] a presenter of *Top Gear*, a famous TV programme about cars and driving. In one show, he [9]_____ [is asked / was asked] an 'ask the host' question about road signs. He [10]_____ [doesn't know / didn't know] the answer!

Vocabulary: words in context

SB p.135

Read the conversation between Anna and her mother. Match the words or the phrase in the box with the gaps in the conversation.

points	speed	has nothing to do with	silly

Mother: What's the matter? Please let me help you.

Anna: No, thank you. It's my problem – it [1]_____ you.

Mother: Now you're being [2]_____ – everyone needs help sometimes.

Anna: OK, but I'm angry because we did a quiz at school today and I didn't get any [3]_____.

Mother: What were the questions about?

Anna: Mostly about the size, weight and [4]_____ of different animals.

Mother: Really! Oh dear! I don't think I'd do well either.

1 Put the words in order to write *Yes / No questions*.

1 you / have / seen / Paul *Have you seen Paul?* _____

2 walking / you / home / are _____

3 catch / did / they / thief / the _____

4 been / she / has / long / waiting _____

5 themselves / are / children / enjoying / the _____

6 got / you / smartphone / a / have _____

2 Put the words in order to write *question-word questions*.

1 to / been / you / who / talking / have *Who have you been talking to?* _____

2 brother / old / your / is / how _____

3 you / standing / where / were _____

4 meaning / this / what / is / the / of _____

5 happened / after / what / yesterday / school _____

6 passed / many / students / how / the / test _____

3 Write the questions.

1 I've finished my work. And you? *Have you finished your work?* _____

2 We're going out. And you? _____

3 I arrived home late yesterday. And you? _____

4 My mother goes to work by taxi. And yours? _____

5 I didn't have breakfast this morning. And you? _____

6 I must go now. And you? _____

4 If this is the answer, what's the question? Write the questions.

Answers	Questions
1 In 1998.	_____
2 *Slumdog Millionaire.*	_____
3 It's played in teams.	_____

Vocabulary: writing crossword clues

Look at the words in the crossword and write the clues.

The crossword contains the following words:

- 4 Across: preposition
- 5 Across: lecture
- 6 Across: waiter
- 7 Across: audience
- 1 Down: confusing
- 2 Down: millionaire
- 3 Down: energy
- 4 Down: publish

Across

4 _____

5 _____

6 _____

7 _____

Down

1 _____

2 _____

3 _____

4 _____

Check your progress

1 What can you do now?

I can ...

- use prepositions and phrases to add meaning to sentences ☐
- write and ask lots of questions ☐
- play some word games ☐
- read and understand part of a story about a game show ☐
- prepare and play *WW2BaM* in a project ☐

2 Answer the questions about this unit.

1 What have you enjoyed most?

_____

2 Is there anything you have found difficult?

_____

3 What would you like to learn more about?

_____

💡 My learning

What did you learn in this unit?

Rivers and bridges

Vocabulary: opposites

Match the opposite adjectives.

long	light
hard	low
heavy	narrow
high	short
large	short
tall	small
wide	soft

long — short

Use of English: past continuous tense   SB p.145

1 Write sentences about what you were doing at different times yesterday.

1 *At six o'clock this morning I was sleeping in bed.*

2 _____

3 _____

4 _____

2 Write sentences about what Helen and Max were doing at the different times.

	Helen	Max
07.00–07.15	get dressed	sleep
07.15–07.30	eat breakfast	get dressed
07.30–08.00	walk to school	eat breakfast / run to school
08.00–15.00	study at school	study at school
16.00–17.00	do dance practice	do football training

1 07:10 / Helen / get dressed *At 07:10 Helen was getting dressed.*

2 07:10 / Max / get dressed *At 07:10 Max wasn't getting dressed. He was sleeping.*

3 07:20 / Helen / get dressed _____

4 07:55 / Max / run to school _____

5 11:00 / Helen / study at school _____

6 11:00 / Max / watch TV _____

7 16:30 / Helen / do dance practice _____

8 16:45 / Max / do dance practice _____

3 Write three yes / no questions about what Helen or Max were doing at different times. Also write short answers.

1 _Was Max eating breakfast at 07:25? No, he wasn't._

2 _____

3 _____

4 _____

4 Write three question-word questions about Helen or Max. Also write full answers.

1 _What was Helen doing at 07:20? She was eating breakfast._

2 _____

3 _____

4 _____

Use of English: present and past continuous passive   SB p.145

All verb tenses can have a passive form.

- We use the *present continuous passive* when we want to say that something is being done by someone for a continuing time in the present. We make it with *am / is / are + being* + past participle.
- We use the *past continuous passive* when we want to say that something was being done by someone for a continuing time in the past. We make it with *was / were + being* + past participle.

Read the A sentences. Write three or four words to complete the B sentences with the passive form of the verb.

1 A They were destroying the bridge when the army arrived.

B The bridge _was being destroyed when the army arrived._

2 A Someone is taking photos.
B Photos _____

3 A They were repairing the computer when it was stolen.
B The computer _____ when it was stolen.

4 A Nobody is cooking the food here now.
B The food _____ here now.

5 A Nobody was building the new bridge when I was there.
B The new bridge _____ when I was there.

6 A Are they painting the house in the rain?
B _____ the house _____ in the rain?

7 A Why were they picking the flowers?
B Why _____ the flowers _____ ?

Reading: comprehension

SB p.147

Read the blog posts again. Are the sentences true or false?

1 The journey started on 25 January.   True / False
2 The journey finished on 17 March.   True / False
3 Anton and Carl made the whole journey in boats.   True / False
4 Anton knows a lot about birds.   True / False
5 Anton is happy that he made the journey.   True / False
6 Anton enjoyed every part of the journey.   True / False

Reading: thinking about the text

SB p.147

1 Which parts of the journey did Anton enjoy the most?

_____

_____

2 Which parts of the journey did Anton enjoy the least?

_____

_____

Vocabulary: words in context

SB p.148

Complete the sentences with words or phrases from the box. Change the form of the verbs, where necessary.

| relax   flow   complain   extremely   mix   look forward to   go by   peace and quiet |

1 After a busy day at work, I need some _____ at home.

2 Having a mobile phone is _____ useful. I don't know what I'd do without it.

3 I am not happy about the food here, so I'm going to _____ to the waiter.

4 I love sitting in a train and watching the countryside _____ .

5 The drink is a _____ of milk and fruit.

6 The river _____ quickly down the hills and then out into the sea.

7 We're all _____ to the summer holidays.

8 You should _____ and stop worrying.

Reading: ordering a story

Read and put the story about Anton in the correct order.

A

The next day he had to return to the shop. The shop assistant said sorry and changed the brown trainer for another green one.

B

The following day he went back to the shoe shop again. This time Anton was very careful. He put on both the trainers in the shop – both green, one left, one right – and put his old shoes in the box. He then walked home in his new shoes. Finally, he had what he wanted!

C

However, when he opened the box at home, he found that he had one green trainer and one brown trainer. He wasn't happy!

D

Anton went shopping before he went on his river journey. He needed some new shoes. He found some green trainers that he liked, so he bought them.

E

When Anton got home, he was furious! He now had two green trainers but they were both for left feet. He still couldn't use them!

1 _____   2 _____   3 _____   4 _____   5 _____

Use of English: connectives

SB p.149

Underline the connectives in the story. Two are done for you.

Remember! Connectives join two ideas in a text.

Read *Focus on History* again and answer the questions.

1 What were the names of the two parts of Egypt in the pre-Kingdom?

_____ _____

2 For about how long did the ancient Egyptians build pyramids? _____

3 What shows us that the ancient Egyptians were happy when the Nile flooded?

_____

4 Name three Egyptian gods or goddesses. _____ _____

_____

5 What stops the River Nile from flooding now? _____

Check your progress

1 **What can you do now?**

I can …

listen to details in descriptions to identify pictures ☐

talk about actions and events continuing in the past ☐

recognise the opinions of the writer in a text, and how opinions can change ☐

use a range of different verb tenses ☐

write a blog post about a journey ☐

2 **Answer the questions about this unit.**

1 What have you enjoyed most?

_____

2 Is there anything you have found difficult?

_____

3 What would you like to learn more about?

_____

My learning

What did you learn in this unit?

Vocabulary: hobbies

SB p.154

Write different lists of hobbies.

Hobbies I have	Hobbies I'd like to have	Hobbies I don't want to have

Reading: comprehension

SB p.155

1 How do we know that extreme ironing became popular quickly?

_____

2 List the sports given in the text which people have done while ironing.

canoeing _____ _____ _____ _____ _____

3 Who was the person who did ironing while running for 21 kilometres?

_____

4 Which country is Scott Wade from?

_____

Reading: thinking about the text

SB p.155

1 Do you think extreme ironing is really a hobby? Is it something anyone can do?

_____

2 What do you think happens when it rains on dirty car art? Do you think the artist is unhappy when this happens?

_____

3 What would you draw on a dirty car window?

_____

Vocabulary: words in context

SB p.156

1 Complete the sentences with the words from the box. Change the form where necessary.

> championship   creative   dust   extraordinary   invent   iron   mobile   smart

1 I can come to see you soon. I'm just _____ my clothes but I've nearly finished.

2 You look very _____ in your new uniform.

3 The World Dog Grooming _____ starts next week.

4 Alexander Graham Bell _____ the telephone in 1876.

5 I just heard an _____ story about a five-year-old boy who got lost in a big city.

6 The house has been empty for six months, so everything is covered in

_____ .

7 My parents have friends who live in a _____ home. They move to a new place every year.

2 Which word from the box is not used? Use this word to write a sentence of your own.

_____

Use of English: relative clauses

SB pp.156–157

A *relative clause* describes a noun. We can use it to make more interesting and longer sentences.

1 Complete the sentences with relative clauses. Leave out pronouns where necessary.

1 I have a friend. He is from Ghana.
I have a friend *who is from Ghana*.

2 I met a friend of my father. He was very funny.
I met a friend of my father _____.

3 I watched a TV programme about extreme ironing. It was fascinating.
I watched a TV programme about extreme ironing _____.

4 She is a friend. She helped me with my homework.
This is the friend _____.

5 Here are some mangoes. I picked them a few minutes ago.
Here are some mangoes _____.

6 The boy broke his leg. He was in the other team.
The boy _____ was in the other team.

2 Rewrite into one longer sentence with a relative clause.

1 My sister bought some new shoes. They were very expensive.
My sister bought some new shoes which were very expensive.

2 Juan has found a hobby website. It contains lots of interesting information.

_____

3 Do you remember my neighbour? He went to the USA five years ago.

_____

4 My father bought a mobile phone last week. It doesn't work properly.

_____

5 You can ask the man for directions. He is standing by the door.

_____

3 Complete the sentences.

1 A dog groomer is someone *who cuts a dog's hair.*

2 An inventor is someone _____.

3 Scott Wade is an artist _____.

4 An art gallery is a place _____.

Vocabulary: words in context

SB p.158

Complete the conversation with the words from the box.

| design | details | outline | rubbed | shape | smooth |

Mother: That looks really beautiful and it smells good, too. I can see it has the ¹_____ of a flower, but what's it made of?

Maria: Soap. It's a soap carving.

Mother: Really! How did you do it?

Maria: Well, first I made a ²_____ on paper, to help me plan what to do. Then I used a pencil to draw the ³_____ of the flower on the soap. Then I started cutting the soap carefully.

Mother: Did it take long?

Maria: About half an hour. At first the outside was rough, so I ⁴_____ it carefully with my hands to make it ⁵_____ . Then I put a bit of water on the top to make it soft and drew some ⁶_____ to make it look better.

Mother: Well, I think it's lovely. Well done!

Use of English: adjective + *to* + verb

SB p.158

After adjectives, *to* + verb is used:

to express an opinion	*Soap carving is easy to do.*
to express a feeling	*I was happy to hear you are feeling better.*

Read the A sentences. Then complete the B sentences using *to* + verb so that they mean the same as the A sentences.

1 A Learning a new language is hard work.

  B It is hard work *to learn a new language.*

2 A I lost my homework. I was silly.

  B I was silly _____.

3 A Finding an interesting hobby is easy.

  B It is easy_____.

4 A Playing computer games is fun.

  B It _____.

5 A Lola said something that wasn't true. That was wrong.

  B Lola was wrong _____.

Use of English: verb + (*–ing* form or *to* + verb)

SB p.158

1 Choose the correct form of the verb to complete the sentences.

1 We hope *to see* you later. [seeing / to see]

2 We all want _____ the end of the story. [knowing / to know]

3 Can you imagine _____ in the future. [living / to live]

4 We decided _____ home because it was late. [going / to go]

5 Don't agree _____ something that you cannot do. [doing / to do]

6 Did he promise _____ us? [helping / to help]

2 Complete the sentences with the verbs from the box. Use the *–ing* form or *to* + verb.

> give   eat   get   sweep   meet

1 I get up at six o'clock every morning. I don't mind _____ up early.

2 Did they agree _____ us after school?

3 Doctors suggest _____ plenty of fruit and vegetables each day.

4 Have you finished _____ the floor yet?

5 They were hot and thirsty, so I offered _____ them a drink.

Vocabulary: *made of*

Are they made of bone, glass, metal, plastic, wire or wood? Complete the sentences.

1 They are made of

_____

2 They are made of

_____

3 They are made of

_____

4 They are made of

_____

5 They are made of

_____

6 They are made of

_____

Check your progress

1 What can you do now?

I can ...

name some hobbies and activities ☐

follow spoken instructions to make something ☐

encourage others to try a hobby ☐

write about a favourite hobby for a website ☐

use relative clauses in sentences ☐

2 Answer the questions about this unit.

1 What have you enjoyed most?

_____

2 Is there anything you have found difficult?

_____

3 What would you like to learn more about?

_____

My learning

What did you learn in this unit?

Space travel

Reading: ordering a text

SB p.166

Read the paragraphs about the history of space travel. Put them in the correct order (1–6).

[ ] A few years later, space travel to the Moon was stopped, but from 1981 to 2011 space shuttles flew into space and back. They were planes that could fly in space. They flew around Earth at 28 000 kilometres per hour.

[ ] The first animal to orbit Earth was a dog called Laika in 1957. Its spacecraft was just 4 metres high.

[ ] In 1986 the first space station was built. A space station is a huge spacecraft that flies around Earth but never returns to land. The International Space Station is still flying 400 kilometres above Earth now, and it will probably be used until 2024.

[ ] Eight years later, in 1969, man first landed on the Moon. That's a journey of 400 000 kilometres there and 400 000 kilometres back! The first astronaut on the Moon was Neil Armstrong, an American. He spent two and a half hours walking and jumping around the Moon.

[1] The first travellers in space were animals. In fact, the very first were insects. In 1947 some flies were sent into space for three minutes. They returned safely to Earth. Two years later, a monkey called Albert became the first mammal in space. He flew 130 kilometres above Earth.

[ ] The first man went into space in 1961. He was a Russian named Yuri Gagarin and he orbited Earth once, which took 108 minutes.

Vocabulary: words in context

Complete the text with the words from the box. Change the form where necessary.

| astronaut   Earth   land   orbit   spacecraft |

The month of July in 1969 was an extraordinary one in the history of space travel. A ¹_____ called Apollo 11 took off on 16 July with three men on board. They travelled for three days before they went into ²_____ around the Moon. Neil Armstrong and Buzz Aldrin then got into a small spacecraft called the *Eagle* to travel to the Moon. They ³_____ on 21 July and spent twenty-one and a half hours on the Moon. During this time, the third ⁴_____, Michael Collins, was flying around the Moon. All three astronauts returned safely to ⁵_____ on 24 July.

The Eagle after take-off from the Moon

Use of English: adjective +preposition

SB p.167

1 Match the two parts of the sentence.

1 My mother's really good	**a** in space travel.
2 Dad's interested	**b** about your holiday?
3 Are you excited	**c** at helping people.
4 I'm keen	**d** for his music or for his acting?
5 The puppy is afraid	**e** of loud noises.
6 Is he more famous	**f** on starting to learn French next year.

2 Complete the sentences with a preposition. Sometimes more than one answer is possible.

1 I'm angry _with him_ for breaking my keyboard.

2 She's angry _____ the broken window.

3 It's very kind _____ you to help me.

4 Are you interested _____ space travel?

5 Don't be afraid _____ the cat – it doesn't scratch.

6 I feel very sorry _____ Pedro because he lost his home.

7 I can't talk to you now as I'm short _____ time.

Reading: comprehension

SB p.168

Write answers to the questions.

1 How high does the ISS fly? _____

2 How fast does the ISS fly, in kilometres per hour? _____

3 Why do things float around on the ISS? _____

4 What happens with water on the ISS? _____

5 What work do the astronauts do on the ISS? _____

Reading: thinking about the text

1 Apart from cleaning their teeth, which other parts of the astronauts' daily routine do you think are difficult for them on the ISS?

_____

2 The astronauts live and work on the ISS for a few months. What work do you think they do when they are at home?

_____

Vocabulary: words in context

SB p.169

1 Complete the sentences with the words from the box.

| crew   experiment   float   gravity   stick   sunrise   sunset   tie |

1 There is no _____ on the Moon, so you can jump a long way.

2 There is always a _____ of six men or women on the ISS.

3 A balloon can _____ and blow around in the wind.

4 Our class did an _____ in science yesterday to show how the wings of a plane help it to fly.

5 Now _____ your picture onto a piece of paper.

6 We watched a beautiful _____ while we sat on the beach in the evening.

7 You need to _____ your shoelace or you might trip.

2 Which word from the box is not used? Use this word to write a sentence of your own.

_____

Use of English: the passive

SB p.170

1 Complete the sentences with the verbs in the present simple passive form.

1 The ISS _____ by the astronauts. [clean]

2 In the ISS, astronauts _____ to the wall when they sleep. [tie]

3 English _____ in Australia. [speak]

4 Many cars _____ in China. [build]

5 How _____ glass _____? [make]

6 Where did you say gold _____? [find]

We often use the *passive form* to talk about something that has been introduced.

> *English is a useful language. It <u>is spoken</u> around the world.*
>
> *Space shuttles are expensive. They <u>are not built</u> any more.*

2 Choose which sentence follows on best, active (A) or passive (P)?

1 The day starts early for the astronauts on the ISS.

~~(A) Someone turns on the lights at six o'clock.~~

(P) The lights are turned on at six o'clock.

2 The new *Toy Story* film is very funny.

(A) They are showing it on television on Saturday.

(P) It is being shown on television on Saturday.

3 My uncle is a pilot.

(A) He has flown all over the world.

(P) The world has been flown all over by him.

4 The internet is one of the most important inventions of recent years.

(A) People use it to communicate across international boundaries.

(P) It is used to communicate across international boundaries.

5 My old school is no longer used.

(A) Workers are pulling it down next week.

(P) It is being pulled down next week.

Vocabulary: jobs   SB p.171

1 Write the name of …

1 … someone who travels in space.   _____

2 … someone who works in science.   _____

3 … someone who looks after animals.   _____

4 … someone who finds out information about a crime. _____

5 … someone who is good at sports, particularly in competitions. _____

6 … someone who works in politics to run a country or area. _____

7 … someone who cuts and looks after hair.   _____

8 … someone who puts out fires and helps people in danger. _____

2 Which names of jobs shown in the word cloud were not described above? Write a sentence about the jobs starting '… someone who …'.

_____

_____

Vocabulary: the planets

Can you find the names of seven planets?

b	q	u	r	a	n	u	s	c	n
m	a	r	s	t	w	s	z	d	e
e	e	q	l	f	d	h	t	n	p
r	f	j	u	p	i	t	e	r	t
c	v	d	p	q	f	s	x	t	u
u	b	r	v	d	g	p	s	g	n
r	n	t	e	g	b	k	w	b	e
y	m	g	n	t	n	j	a	n	g
t	s	k	u	y	m	b	f	h	f
g	a	x	s	a	t	u	r	n	v

Sun
Moon
Mercury
Earth
Saturn
Neptune
Uranus
Pluto
Venus
Mars
Jupiter

Check your progress

1 What can you do now?

I can …

listen to a talk to identify dates and facts ☐

use adjectives and prepositions together ☐

take part in a class discussion about jobs ☐

write giving reasons to explain an opinion ☐

work out how much I weigh on other planets ☐

2 Answer the questions about this unit.

1 What have you enjoyed most?

_____

2 Is there anything you have found difficult?

_____

3 What would you like to learn more about?

_____

My learning

What did you learn in this unit?

Reading: finding specific information

SB pp.176–177

Complete the table with information from the text.

prediction	when predicted	who by *or* in what	when it came true
journey to the Moon			

Reading: thinking about the text

SB pp.176–177

Write your predictions to answer these questions from the text. Give reasons for your answers.

1 Will there be flying cars? _____

_____

2 Will we live on other planets? _____

_____

3 Will there be homes under the sea? _____

_____

Vocabulary: words in context

SB p.177

1 Complete the sentences with the words from the box.

apart   available   common   interest   invent   prediction

1 Breakfast is _____ from 6.30 a.m.

2 My _____ is that we will all use driverless cars by 2030.

3 Talking on a mobile phone is a _____ cause of road accidents.

4 My friend showed a lot of _____ in going to the science fiction fair in London.

5 We lived with my grandparents for many years, but we live _____ now – about 20 km away.

2 Which word from the box is not used? Use this word to write a sentence of your own.

_____

Use of English: quantity

SB p.177

Complete the sentences with the phrases from the box.

> all of the people   both his arms   one third of our lives
> some of the time   three times a day

1 Anton fell off a horse and broke _____.

2 _____, I worry about what will happen in the future.

3 I have to take this medicine _____.

4 It's not possible to make _____ happy all of the time.

5 We spend _____ asleep.

Vocabulary: words in context

SB p.179

1 Read what Gavin said. Then match the words in bold with their meanings.

'When I was little, I used to **copy** Mum and Dad filling a **saucepan** with water. But I never knew you should turn the **tap** off, and the water used to **overflow** and my **sleeves** got **soaked**.'

1 a cooking pot, usually with a handle and a top _____

2 something (often in a kitchen or a bathroom) used to control how much water comes out _____

3 the part of clothes that cover your arms _____

4 to come over the top of something because there is too much of it

_____

5 to try to do what someone else does _____

6 very wet _____

2 Complete the sentences with the words from the box.

> complicated   database   knowledge   professor   robot   task

1 A computer has to search its _____ very quickly.

2 I don't know what to do. This problem is very _____ .

3 My _____ was to clean the kitchen after everyone had finished cooking.

4 My cousin is a _____ of mathematics at a university in England.

5 Our sports teacher has a lot of _____ and experience of many sports.

6 The story is about a talking _____ that can do everything in a house.

Use of English: making predictions

SB p.179

will + verb is used for making predictions about the future. It is often used with *I think* ...

> *I think robots will do all housework in the future.*

Write five predictions about the future.

_____

_____

_____

_____

_____

_____

_____

_____

_____

_____

Use of English: talking about timetabled events

SB p.180

The present simple tense is used for things that are timetabled to happen in the future.

> *His plane arrives at 08:30. What time does the exam begin tomorrow?*

Make sentences. Write: statements ☑, negative statements [X] or questions [?].

the film / start / at 19:00 ☑   *The film starts at 19:00.*

the exams / begin / next week [X]   *The exams don't begin next week.*

what time / the show / start [?]   *What time does the show start?*

1 school / finish / early tomorrow ☑ _____

2 what time / the train / arrive [?] _____

3 we / have / a meeting / next month [X] _____

4 when / the next lesson / start [?] _____

5 the bank / close / at / 15:00 on Fridays ☑ _____

6 this bus / go / past the school [X] _____

The present continuous tense is used for fixed plans – often with a time, date or place.

I'm meeting him at six o'clock at the airport. They're arriving on Monday.

1 Robby is a robot that works for a family. Read the plans for next week and complete the sentences.

1 On Sunday Robby *is driving* the family to the beach.

2 On Sunday evening he _____ the car.

3 On Monday morning he _____ the children to school.

4 On Tuesday evening he _____ the family to a restaurant.

2 Correct the statements.

1 On Monday evening Robby is ~~cleaning the house~~. *cooking a meal*

2 On Wednesday morning he is repairing the hoverbike. _____

3 On Friday evening he is cooking a meal. _____

4 On Saturday morning he is shutting down and updating his database. _____

3 Write three more sentences about the plans for Robby.

_____

_____

_____

4 Imagine that a friend has made plans to go away on a holiday. Write the questions to ask about his / her plans.

1 where /go   *Where are you going?* _____

2 when / leave _____

3 who / you / go / with _____

4 when / come / home _____

<u>Sunday</u>

day – drive family to beach

evening – clean car

<u>Monday</u>

morning – take children to school

afternoon – clean house

evening – cook a meal

<u>Tuesday</u>

day – repair the hoverbike

evening – drive family to restaurant

<u>Wednesday</u>

day – look after baby

evening – clean house

<u>Thursday</u>

day – gardening

evening – cook a meal

<u>Friday</u>

day – check computers in house are working

evening – go shopping

<u>Saturday</u>

day – iron clothes

evening – shut down and update database

Vocabulary: writing crossword clues

Read the words in the crossword and write the clues.

The crossword contains the following answers:

Across: 2 task, 4 common, 5 apart, 6 available, 7 fiction, 8 predict

Down: 1 c o m m a c a t e (vertical letters: c, m, m, a, c, a, e), 3 knowledge

Across

2 _____

4 _____

5 _____

6 _____

7 _____

8 _____

Down

1 _____

3 _____

Check your progress

1 What can you do now?

I can …

listen to part of a story and understand what the characters are discussing ☐

make predictions about the future ☐

talk about the future using four different verb forms ☐

discuss, plan, write, edit and revise a story ☐

work out the meaning of new words in a literature text ☐

My learning
What did you learn in this unit?

2 Answer the questions about this unit.

1 What have you enjoyed most?

_____

2 Is there anything you have found difficult?

_____

3 What would you like to learn more about?

_____

End-of-year review

Vocabulary: word hunt

Write three words that are:

- the names of hobbies
- the names of rivers
- the names of insects
- the names of healthy foods
- verbs followed by –ing form of a verb
- verbs followed by to + verb.

_____ _____ _____
_____ _____ _____
_____ _____ _____
_____ _____ _____
_____ _____ _____
_____ _____ _____

Vocabulary: a crossword

Follow the clues to complete the crossword puzzle.

Across

1 to break something so that it cannot be used again

7 good at understanding, learning and thinking

8 a group of the same things that come one after the other

9 the people who work together, usually on a ship or plane

10 an abstract noun – the feeling of being happy

Down

2 being flat with no holes or edges – the opposite of rough

3 to keep healthy you need a _____ diet

4 a number you use to count the score in a game or sport

5 very small

6 to make someone more likely to do something

Writing: punctuation

Rewrite the sentences, correcting the mistakes.

1 gavin his father and the professor were talking about robots

_____

2 the professor laughed. "can you remember what robots were first used for, in the twentieth century

_____

_____

3 I know said Gavin. working in factories making cars and fridges, those sorts of things"

_____

4 do you know how long it took us scientists to build a robot that can see and hear and reason and move around asked the professor

_____

_____

Writing: silent letters

Some words have letters that we do not pronounce. We call these silent letters (for example, _knife_, _wrong_).

1 Circle the silent letter in each of these words.

1 write	**2** sign	**3** comb	**4** foreign
5 island	**6** biscuit	**7** fascinating	**8** cupboard

2 Find the words with silent letters and write them. Then circle the silent letters.

1 It's the day after Tuesday. _____

2 It comes between summer and winter. _____

3 You use them to cut paper and material. _____

4 It's where you study. _____

5 It's a baby cow. _____

6 It's where your body keeps food after you eat. _____

7 It's what you should do when you are asked a question. _____

8 You have to do this to get up a mountain. _____

Focus on grammar

1 Present continuous tense

a. The present continuous tense
   - is made with *am / is / are* + *–ing* form of the verb
   - is used to talk about actions that are continuing in the present
   - is also used to talk about future plans (see *Section 4* below)

2 Past continuous tense

b. The past continuous tense
   - is made with *was / were* + *–ing* form of the verb
   - is used to talk about actions that were continuing in the past. It is often used with a time or another finished action or event in the past (i.e. the past simple tense).

3 Present perfect tense

The present perfect tense

- is made with *have / has* (*not*) + the past participle of the verb
- links the past and the present. The action takes place in the past but there is always a connection with *now*.

The present perfect tense has three uses:

a. for something that has happened recently

   We sometimes use *just* when we talk about the recent past.

   The players have just arrived.

b. for something that started in the past and is still not finished

   We often use *for* and *since* when we talk about the unfinished past.
   - Use *since* with a point in time.

     Scientists have known about Komodo dragons since 1916.
   - Use *for* with a period of time.

     They have studied these strange creatures for over a hundred years.

c. for an experience

   We often use *ever* in questions and *never* in answers when we talk about experiences.

   Have you ever seen a Komodo dragon?

   No, I've never seen one in real life but I've seen them on television.

4 Future forms

There are four ways to talk about the future in English:

She	*will arrive*	*tomorrow evening at 19:00.*
	is going to arrive	
	is arriving	
	arrives	

All of the sentences are correct. However, there are some differences in the use of each.

a. **will** + verb is used for

- sudden decisions (often with *I think*)

  I think I'll talk to my teacher tomorrow.
  I'm tired. I think I'll go to bed.

- predicting or guessing

  In the future we will all go to university.
  I think it will rain tomorrow.

- future events you are certain about

  It will be my birthday next week.
  The teacher will be here in a minute.

b. **be going to** + verb is used for

- something we have decided to do, or plans

  I'm going to fly to Lagos tomorrow.
  He's going to visit us on Friday.

- future events we have evidence for

  Look at the sky! It's going to rain.
  Look at the time! We're going to be late.

c. The **present continuous tense** is used for

- fixed or firm plans – often with a time, date or place

  I'm meeting him at six o'clock at the airport.
  They're arriving on Monday.

d. The **present simple tense** is used for

- things which are timetabled to happen in the future

  His plane arrives at 08:30.
  What time does the exam begin tomorrow?

5 Passive forms

- A passive can be used with any of the verb tenses: we use the verb *be* in the appropriate tense + the past participle. Here are some examples:

PRESENT SIMPLE PASSIVE:	The film	is	chosen	by the manager.
PRESENT CONTINUOUS PASSIVE:	The book	is being	written.	
PAST SIMPLE PASSIVE:	The car	was	washed	by my sister.
PAST CONTINUOUS PASSIVE:	We	were being	followed.	
PRESENT PERFECT PASSIVE:	A dog	has been	found.	

- We use passives when we don't know, we don't want to say, or it is not important who did something. Passives are often used in reports.

  My money was stolen. (I don't know who took it.)

  A window has been broken. (I don't want to say that I broke it.)

  A lot of rice is eaten in Asia. (It is not important who eats it.)

- When we use a passive and want to say who did something, we use *by* …

  A telephone call was made by my mother.

6 Modal verbs

- Modal verbs add meaning to main verbs. They are not used when referring to facts. They are used to express ability, possibility, certainty, requests, suggestions, necessity, and so on.
- The modal verbs are: *can, could, may, might, must, shall, should, will, would, ought to*. We also use *have to* and *need to* for the same purpose.
- We use modal verbs before main verbs and in short answers.
  You must hurry up. Can you wait a minute? No, I can't.
- Modal verbs only have one form (they do not add *–s*, *–ing* or *–ed*).
- After a modal we use the simple form of the main verb.
  You may go.
  We should wait.
- Modal verbs do not need *do / does / did* in questions.
  Could you help me? (NOT ~~Do you could help me?~~)

7 General and likely conditionals (zero and first conditionals)

- Conditional sentences have two parts, or clauses. One of the clauses usually starts with *if*. The two clauses can go in either order. When the *if*-clause is first, we use a comma between the two clauses.
- We can replace *if + not* with *unless*.
  If it isn't safe, I won't take you. = Unless it is safe, I won't take you.

The general conditional

- has both clauses in the present simple tense (or one in the present simple tense and the other in the imperative)
- is used to talk about the results of things which are always true.
  If you heat water to 100°C, it boils.
  It is very hot here if the sun shines.

The likely conditional

- has one clause in the present simple tense and the other clause in the future tense with *will* + verb
- is used to talk about the results of things which are likely to happen.
  If it rains tomorrow, we will have the party inside.
  I will see you on Monday unless you are still ill.

8 Reported speech

- When we use reported speech, the place, time and speaker has usually changed from the time and place that the words were spoken. For this reason we often have to change the verb tenses, pronouns and 'time and place' words.
- The tenses change like this:

tense change	speaking	reported speech
present simple → past simple	"I **walk** to school."	He said he **walked** to school.
present continuous → past continuous	"He **is working**."	She said he **was working**.
past simple → past perfect	"I **played** football."	He said he **had played** football.
present perfect → past perfect	"We **have missed** school every day."	I said we **had missed** school every day.

- Examples of how time and place words change:

now	→	then
today	→	that day
yesterday	→	the day before
tomorrow	→	the next day
next week / month / year	→	the following week / month / year
last week / month / year	→	the week / month / year before
here	→	there

- When we report on a situation that has not changed (the time and place are still the same), then we do not have to change the verb tense. This happens when

  ○ we repeat something immediately after it is said

  "He is arriving soon." "What did you say?" "I said he is arriving soon."

  ○ we are talking about something which is still true or always true

  "My name is William."   *He said his name is William.*

  "Water boils at 100 °C."   *The teacher told us that water boils at 100 °C.*

- The most common verbs for reporting are *said* and *told*. There is an important difference in the way they are used.

  ○ We use *told* when we say **who** somebody is talking to.

  *Adu **told his wife** that there was a problem.*   *I told **you** that I would help.*

  ○ We use *said* in other cases.

  Adu said that there was a problem.   *I said that we would meet later.*

- To report a command, use *told* + noun / pronoun + *to* + verb.

  The teacher said, "Cal, sit down."   *The teacher told Cal to sit down.*

- To report a request, use *asked* + noun / pronoun + *to* + verb.

  Jan said, "Help me carry this box, please." Jan asked me to help him carry a box.

- To report a *Wh-question*, use *asked* and the word order of a statement (not a question). Do not use a question mark.

  He said, "Where are you going?"   *The man asked where I was going.*

- To report a *yes / no* question, use *asked + if.*

  My mother said, "Are you feeling well?"   *My mother asked if I was feeling well.*

9 Relative clauses

- Relative clauses are used to give information about a noun. They allow us to make sentences longer and more interesting.
- There are two types of relative clause.

  a. A **defining relative clause** tells us who or what the noun is. It is an important part of a sentence. If we take it out we might not know which noun we are talking about.

  *The doctor **who you saw yesterday** is away today.*

  b. A **non-defining relative clause** gives us extra information about the noun. We can take it out of the sentence and still understand it. We use commas to separate it from the rest of the sentence.

  *The doctor, **who is now over 70**, is resting.*

- The first word of a relative clause is usually a relative pronoun.
  - **who** – refers to a person
    *I saw a man **who** has a wooden leg.*
  - **which** – refers to an animal or a thing
    *There is the monkey **which** bit me.*
  - **that** – can replace *who* and *which* to refer to a person, animal or thing
    *I saw a man **that** has a wooden leg.*   *There is the monkey **that** bit me.*
- Relative pronouns replace other pronouns in the relative clause – don't use both.
  My mother has a friend who ~~she~~ is a singer.
- We can use *why* in a relative clause to give reasons.
  *The reason **why** I like her is that she always has time to help.*

10 Question forms

- Yes / no questions do not include a question word and can be answered with *yes* or *no*. They all have an auxiliary, modal or the main verb *be* (*am, is, are, was, were*) before the subject.
- Use the same auxiliary or modal as in the statement form.

  *He **has** seen us.*   *We **can** wait here.*   *He **is** late.*

  ***Has** he seen us?*   ***Can** we wait here?*   *Is he late?*
- The main verb follows the subject.

  *They are **watching** us.*   *Are they **watching** us? ~~Are watching they us?~~*
- If there are two auxiliary verbs in the statement, put only the first before the subject.

  *He **has been** sleeping.*   ***Has** he **been** sleeping? ~~Has been he sleeping?~~*
- For present simple tense questions use *do* or *does* + verb.

  We leave home before 8 o'clock.   ***Do** you **leave** home before 8 o'clock?*
- For past simple questions use *did* + verb.

  We watched the football game last night.   ***Did** you **watch** the football game last night?*
- Question-word questions start with a question word: *why, what, which, when, where* or *how*. The word order after the question word is usually the same as for yes / no questions.

QUESTION WORD	AUXILIARY / MODAL	SUBJECT	VERB
When	*can*	*you*	*start?*
Where	*is*	*your brother*	*studying?*

- The question words *who, what, which* and *how much / many* can be used to ask questions about a subject or an object. When the question is asked about the object, we use an auxiliary or modal before the subject as usual. When the question is asked about the subject, we do not use an auxiliary or modal and the word order is the same as for a statement.

SUBJECT	VERB	OBJECT	
Kalu	*told*	*Sani.*	*Who did Kalu tell?* (Sani, OBJECT)
			Who told Sani? (Kalu, SUBJECT)
The cat	*is chasing*	*the mouse.*	*What is the cat chasing?* (the mouse, OBJECT)
			What is chasing the mouse? (the cat, SUBJECT)

11 *to + verb* after adjectives and verbs

- After adjectives, we use *to + verb*.
  I'm happy to see you.   It is important to stay healthy.   It isn't easy to understand this book.
- After some verbs, we use *to + verb*.
  I hope to see you later.   *I'm planning to start my own blog.*

12 *–ing* forms after prepositions and verbs

- After a preposition, we use the *–ing* form of a verb.
  Thank you for helping.   *Are you bored of doing the same old things?*
- After some verbs, we use the *–ing* form of a verb.
  I enjoyed talking to you.   *Can you imagine living in the future?*

13 *–ing* forms as subject and object

We can use the *–ing* form of the verb as a noun. This can be the subject or object of the sentence.
Swimming is good exercise.   *I enjoy running.*

14 Adjective + preposition

- Some adjectives are followed by prepositions. Using a different preposition sometimes changes the meaning.
  I'm angry with my little brother.   *I'm angry about the noise he's making.*

15 Participles as adjectives

- We can use the present and the past participles of some verbs as adjectives.
- Those made from present participles (ending in *–ing*) often describe the cause of a feeling.
- Those made from past participles (ending in *–ed*) often describe the feeling.
  This book is boring.   *I am bored because of this book.*

16 Pronouns

- Pronouns are used in place of nouns. They are:

Subject pronouns	I	you	he	she	it	we	you (pl)	they
Object pronouns	me	you	him	her	it	us	you (pl)	them
Possessive adjectives	my	your	his	her	its	our	your (pl)	their
Possessive pronouns	mine	yours	his	hers	-	ours	yours (pl)	theirs
Reflexive pronouns	myself	yourself	himself	herself	itself	ourselves	yourselves	themselves

- The pronoun *you* can be used to mean 'people in general'.

- Pronouns take the place of nouns, for example: *she, it, them, ours.*
- We use indefinite pronouns when we don't know, or don't want to say, exactly who or what we are talking about.
- The indefinite pronouns are:

everybody	everyone	everything
somebody	someone	something
anybody	anyone	anything
nobody	no one	nothing

- The reciprocal pronouns are *each other* and *one another*. We use them when two or more people do the same thing.
- *They love each other. They all help one another with their projects.*

17 Quantifiers

- Quantifiers are small words that tell us about quantity, for example: *some, many, a few.*
- Some quantifiers can be used only with countable nouns and some only with uncountable nouns. Others can be used with both.

Countable			Uncountable		
How many eggs do we have?			*How much money do we have?*		
We have	a large number of a lot of/lots of plenty of many some a few/several not many	eggs.	We have	a large amount of a lot of/lots of plenty of much some a little not much	money.

- We can use words like *all of, half of, twice,* to tell us more information about amount.
  We have been waiting all this time.   *Half of my money was stolen.*

18 Comparing

- When we compare with adjectives, we can make the comparison stronger or weaker by using structures like *not as* + adjective + *as* or *much* + comparative adjective + *than.*
  I'm not as tall as you.   He's much stronger than he was.   She's much more helpful than she was.
- When we compare with adverbs, we can make the comparison stronger or weaker by using structures like *not as* + adverb + *as* or *far less / more* + adverb.
  This computer doesn't work as quickly as it used to.
  You drive far more carefully than your father.
- We use *like* or *as* to say one thing is the same as another. These are called similes.
  - verb + *like* + noun phrase: *She's like a second mother to me.*
    It disappeared like ice in the sun.
  - *as* + adjective + *as*: *It was as cold as ice.*
    He ran as fast as a cheetah.

19 Noun phrases

- We can use a group of words to act like a noun. This adds interest and information to sentences.
- A noun phrase can be replaced by a pronoun.

  I ate a large pile of delicious sandwiches. [I ate them.]

20 Prepositional phrases

- We can add interest and meaning to a sentence by using preposition + phrase.
- These prepositional phrases can go at the beginning, middle or end of a sentence.

  <u>At the start</u>, I didn't have many friends.

  We were stopped <u>by the owners of the shop</u> before we went in.

  People visit from <u>around the world</u>.

21 Connectives

- Conjunctions connect two ideas in a sentence.
  - Some always go between the two ideas, for example: *and, or, but, so.*
  - Others can go between the two ideas or at the beginning of the sentence. If the conjunction is at the beginning of the sentence, use a comma between the two ideas.

    Although I like flying, I didn't enjoy that journey.
- We use *as* and *since* for giving a reason. They are more formal than *because.*

  As / Since you like football, I'm going to take you to a match on Saturday.

  We'll leave her in the morning as / since it will be very busy later.
- We use *so … that* and *such … that* to give a reason or explanation. They have the same meaning.
  - We use *so … that* with an adjective or adverb.

    I'm so happy that I saw you.   *They were running so fast that they couldn't stop.*
  - We use *such … that* with a noun (or adjective + noun).

    It's such a pity that I didn't see you.   *I've had such a bad day that I just want to go to bed.*
- Some useful connectives are:

used for	Connective
time	when, before, after, as soon as, the next day / week / month / year
order or sequence	first, then, next, finally
examples	for example, for instance, in the same way
extra information	also, in addition, apart from that
explanations, reasons and results	because, such as, so, therefore, as, as a result, for this reason
contrast	but, however, although, on the other hand
concluding	in conclusion, in summary, to sum up